ANSWERING
THE CALL

THE JOURNEYS TO LEADERSHIP SERIES

The "Journeys to Leadership" series is about successful women who have reached the pinnacle of their careers. It features stories about extraordinary women who have found paths to success—whether it's leading a college or university, becoming successful scholars in science and engineering, or thriving in some other male-dominated arena.

Available:

Women at the Top
What Women University and College Presidents Say
About Effective Leadership

Forthcoming:

Latinas in the Workplace
An Emerging Leadership Force

ANSWERING THE CALL

AFRICAN AMERICAN WOMEN IN HIGHER EDUCATION LEADERSHIP

Beverly L. Bower *and* Mimi Wolverton

Sty/us

STERLING, VIRGINIA

Sty/us

COPYRIGHT © 2009 BY STYLUS PUBLISHING, LLC.

Published by Stylus Publishing, LLC
22883 Quicksilver Drive
Sterling, Virginia 20166–2102

Library of Congress Cataloging-in-Publication-Data
Bower, Beverly L.
  Answering the call : African American women in
higher education leadership / Beverly L. Bower and
Mimi Wolverton.—1st ed.
    p. cm.— (Pathways to leadership)
  Includes bibliographical references and index.
  ISBN 978-1-57922-253-6 (hardcover : alk. paper)—
  ISBN 978-1-57922-254-3 (pbk. : alk. paper)
    1. African American women college administrators.
    I. Wolverton, Mimi.   II. Title.
LB2341.B625   2009
371.1′11082—dc22

                                        2008054642

13-digit ISBN: 978–1-57922–253–6 (cloth)
13-digit ISBN: 978–1-57922–254–3 (paper)

Printed in the United States of America

All first editions printed on acid free paper that meets
the American National Standards Institute Z39–48
Standard.

Bulk Purchases

Quantity discounts are available for use in
workshops and for staff development.
Call 1–800–232–0223

First Edition, 2009

10   9   8   7   6   5   4   3   2   1

To sisters throughout the academy
Lifting as we climb

CONTENTS

Contents

ACKNOWLEDGMENTS

Special thanks to contributors Anneli Adams and Angela Hernquist for sharing work from their dissertations; to our colleague, Wanda Costen, for her contributions to the original research project; to our publisher, John von Knorring, for his support of and belief in our work; and to the hardworking staff at Stylus for all their assistance.

FOREWORD

Answering the Call is the second book in the **Journeys to Leadership** series. The series features stories about extraordinary women who have found paths to success—whether leading a college or university, or becoming successful scholars in science and engineering, or thriving in some other male-dominated arena.

This book follows on the heels of the series' inaugural offering, *Women at the Top*, which highlights the stories of nine college and university presidents. *Answering the Call* looks again at higher education leadership, but its authors distinguish this volume from its predecessor in two distinct ways. First, they expand the general category of women leaders beyond college presidents to include women who work in the policy arena. Second, the book recounts the stories of seven African American women, a narrow segment of an already elite group of leaders—women. Five of the women whose stories are told in *Answering the Call* are, or have been, college presidents; three have devoted a good portion of their lives to leadership in higher education policy venues at state and/or national levels.

Each of these women has been the first woman, or first African American, or first African American woman in one or more of the positions of authority she has held. They are pioneers. They are seasoned. They are successful. They've paid their dues. As

Lois Carson, the oldest woman in the group of seven, might say, "We are trailblazers, and we have the scars to prove it."

We invite you to join us in celebrating these exceptional women, their lives, and their careers. We hope their stories will inspire others to follow in their footsteps. We assure you they will raise questions about today's continued disparity between rhetoric and reality when it comes to the presence of African American women in higher education leadership.

Mimi Wolverton, Series Editor
Pathways to Leadership

one

THE REALITIES OF AFRICAN AMERICAN WOMEN IN HIGHER EDUCATION LEADERSHIP

SINCE THE WOMEN'S MOVEMENT of the 1960s, women have made inroads into the top ranks of leadership in higher education. The American Council on Education's (ACE) 2007 report on the American college presidency indicated that, although progress had slowed in recent years, from 1986 to 2006 the proportion of presidents who were women more than doubled, from 10 percent to 23 percent. Likewise, ACE's 21st annual report on minorities in higher education noted that between 1994 and 2004, minorities made "significant gains" at the presidential level, with appointments of Latino and Black women to the presidency nearly doubling (Harvey & Anderson, 2005). But when progress is measured from an all-but-zero base, the reality is that very few minority women have attained the presidency in the last 20 to 25 years.

By 1990, 133 higher education institutions were led by African Americans, only 18 of whom were women. In 1998, 38 African American women served as college or university presidents, almost all in community colleges or historically Black institutions

(Hamilton, 2004). The 2007 membership directory of the Presidents' Round Table of the National Council on Black American Affairs (an affiliate of the American Association of Community Colleges) includes 40 women community college presidents/ CEOs. Today, 22% of the nation's 120 historically/predominantly Black institutions are led by African American women, but only 8 predominantly White, 4-year institutions have African American women at the helm.

Clearly, the seven African American women whose stories you are about to read represent a unique segment of the population of higher education leaders. Five of these women currently serve or have served as institutional presidents. Three have served in governing/policy positions at the institutional, state, or national level. All four of the five presidents who were serving in that role at the time (Marvalene Hughes, Yolanda Moses, Jerry Sue Thornton, and Belle Wheelan) were recognized in 1999 by *Black Issues in Higher Education* as 20th-century presidents who have influenced the higher education landscape. The list of honors and awards these seven women have received is monumental. Most of them are pioneers in that they have been the first woman, or the first African American, or the first African American woman, in one or more of their leadership positions.

These women are unique not only because of the low numbers of African American women in higher education leadership but because of their undeniable success in the field, as demonstrated by their longevity. Together, they represent nearly 100 years of executive leadership/governance in higher education. Along the way, they have overcome the double-bind of sexism and racism that can inhibit the professional attainment of African American women, particularly as they move toward the top of their professions. Jerry Sue Thornton, for example, reluctantly left Chicago because she recognized at that time that Illinois was not open to accepting women or minorities as college presidents. Belle Wheelan broke through the gender barrier when she was one of the first women to join the Rotary Club in Portsmouth, Virginia. As the first African American woman trustee of San Bernardino Community College, Lois Carson fought to convince her six male colleagues on the District Board of the necessity of campus child care centers. These seven women are successful because they do not accept the limitations of racism and sexism that others say the double-bind imposes.

Although their pathways into leadership are different, there are definite similarities in their experiences, values, and beliefs. Ranging in age from mid-50 to 70-something, each of them has memories of the pre-civil rights era and has experienced first-hand the societal changes that movement brought about for minorities and for women. Their values and ideals were forged in that struggle and/or shaped by the freedom it brought. Belle Wheelan, Debra Austin, and Lois Carson each spent childhood years in the South and attended segregated schools. Lois Carson tells us, "I grew up in a very segregated south, in Memphis, Tennessee. Everything was segregated: schools, buses, restrooms, theaters, and drinking fountains." Sitting with her family watching television, Yolanda Moses remembers Dr. Martin Luther King Jr. delivering his *I Have a Dream* speech. A self-described "child of the sixties," Belle Wheelan declares that "living through two revolutions, a black revolution and a women's revolution," has definitely shaped her beliefs.

Even though the civil rights and women's movements kicked open doors for two previously excluded groups, it didn't mean the welcome mat was out. The entry of African Americans and women into traditional settings, such as college and the workplace, brought with it isolation and systemic discrimination. Born in 1954, Beverly Tatum describes herself as an "integration baby": "I was the only Black kid in the class, one of the few Black children in the school." This experience and the feelings it produced eventually prompted Tatum to study racial identity theory, shaped her role as an "antiracist educator," and provided the focus of her academic career and writing.

African Americans and women still struggle to see their viewpoints and talents valued in American society. "As an ethnic minority and a female, I'm always conscious of the fact that those are the first two things people notice about me when I walk in a room . . . those preconceived notions will be there, ready to be validated by whatever I say," states Belle Wheelan who, as secretary of education for the Commonwealth of Virginia, saw how differences in "gender, ethnicity, SES [socioeconomic status]" can get in the way of making needed change. Her belief in the ability to work through these differences was instilled by her eighth-grade teacher at the all-Black Catholic school she attended, a teacher who demanded the best from her students and inspired them with the notion, "[I]t didn't matter what color our skin was because we were all Americans and 'American' ended in the letters i-c-a-n, I can."

In some ways the challenge of being a woman outweighs the challenge of being African American. "The college presidency is still a male-dominated activity," says Beverly Tatum. According to Debra Austin, the "do this at all cost because there's only one model of success" mindset is the problem. As Belle Wheelan notes, "For women, career choices still revolve more around family than they do for men." Tatum agrees: "Women do face unique challenges—family, childrearing, and marital status. If you have a family, it can be formidable. Because my husband has been such a great partner and a devoted father, I have been able to balance being a mother and having a very demanding career."

Not all of the women have been as fortunate. Some have witnessed the dissolution of their colleagues' marriages, as well as their own, including Belle Wheelan, who has been a single parent since her son was ten months old. She says, "It wasn't easy to have a career and raise a child at the same time. It made for very long days."

These women have persevered, bolstered by the strength and confidence instilled in each of them by parents and early role models. Several of them suggested that their leadership skills were born out of their childhood experiences. From her training in counseling and her personal experience, Marvalene Hughes tells us, "[M]essages from our parents are very important in building confidence and a sense of competence." The message from Yolanda Moses's father to his four daughters was clear: "My father just expected us all to get out there and do something and not to be shy about it. The fact that we were females didn't matter. His position was, 'If you want things to happen; you've got to make them happen.'" For African Americans, women and men alike, succeeding in a society that devalued their abilities in many ways depended on believing in the message that parents, like those of Marvalene Hughes, imparted to their children—"You must be twice as good, but, yes, you can do it." These women exude strength and self-confidence. There is nothing they can't accomplish. They each believe, as Belle Wheelan puts it, "With a little heart and a lot of learning I can do anything."

National demographic data indicate that a significant turnover in college leadership will occur in the near future, presenting increased opportunities for women and minorities who desire and are prepared to be effective higher education leaders. We share the stories of these seven African American women with the hope that their successes, their strategies, their wisdom, their experiences, and, most of all, their passion will inspire the next generation of women to answer the leadership call.

In telling their stories, we combine first- and third-person perspectives. The former allows the reader to listen directly to these women. We narrate their stories to move them along, but each woman tells her own story in her own words. Each story's final rendering was created from the individual's personal recollections, speeches, institutional websites, and newspaper and journal articles written about her. We omitted in-text references because we believe they intrude on the story being told. At the end of each chapter we provide a brief bibliographical note highlighting the primary resources used in telling that particular story. The last chapter includes a detailed explanation of the research process used to generate these stories.

BIBLIOGRAPHICAL NOTE

Data reported in this chapter were compiled from the following sources:

American Council on Education. (2007). *The American college president*. Washington, DC: Author.

American Council on Education. (2008). *The presidency: Special supplement*. Washington, DC: Author.

Hamilton, K. (2004, June 17). The best is yet to come. *Black Issues in Higher Education, 21*(9), 60–64

Harvey, W. B., & Anderson, E. L. (2005). *Minorities in higher education 2003–2004: Twenty-first annual status report*. Washington, DC: American Council on Education

National Council on Black American Affairs. (2007). *The president's roundtable membership directory*. Washington, DC: Author.

two

BEING OKAY WITH BEING ME

Debra Austin

"THERE IS AN OLD ADAGE that says it's lonely at the top. I'd say that leaders tend to be alone rather than lonely. Being lonely connotes something is missing, or sad, or pitiful. It's really not that. We are simply alone. Often, we make decisions alone. We gather input from people around us, but the decision is really up to us. And, when 'the shit hits the fan,' pardon the phrase, it is the leader who is held accountable. You can't share the responsibility with anybody. It ultimately rests with you.

"It's critical to have two or three people with whom you can have frank conversations; whether it's just a whine, W-H-I-N-E, at a wine party [laughing] or a sharing of information. My staff doesn't need to hear me say I don't know what we're going to do. It does not engender confidence. With a peer I trust, I can say, 'I really don't know how to do this. Can you give me some ideas?' And there is no judgment, there is no, 'How incompetent can you be?' But, rather, there is support and a generating of possible solutions to my problems.

"For women in any career, being alone is complicated further by a general cultural insensitivity toward the need for balance. There are some professions that appear to require a total commitment to that career—but at what sacrifice? That 'do this at all cost because there's only one model of success' mindset, I think, is troublesome for women in any area.

"Over the years, I have tried to make a distinction between what I do at work and who I am as a person. I want folks around me who can also make that distinction. It's hard to do sometimes because our culture has created us as extensions of our work, and that's very dangerous because work is fleeting. When people are laid off, their jobs are gone. Those who saw work as themselves no longer feel valued or important. I do a job, I am passionate about a job, I have a vision for my job, but the job is not who I am as a person. Jobs come and go. I can't have my personality coming and going based on jobs [laughing]; I don't think it's emotionally healthy. Debra Austin, Chancellor, is not my name. I am Debra Austin, a person, who happened to play the role of chancellor, who played previous roles and will engage in future ones, who is also Mrs. Kenneth Austin. But first and foremost," she laughs, "I'm my own person. I think leaders have to be able to draw that distinction."

Throughout her career Debra has worked at keeping a balance between her career and her personal life. "I talk with staff about taking personal time because I believe in a balanced approach to work and life. It's important that they take care of themselves. I'd much rather have individuals who attempt to balance their lives than people who are so committed to the organization that they forget their personal lives. I expect them to model that behavior in their own lives and to instill it in their folks, in their staff."

She credits part of her success in balancing work and family to the good fortune of finding a competent and reliable teenage babysitter who stayed with the family for six years while she completed a bachelor's and a master's degree. She was an indispensable part of the family. As a chief academic officer and as an executive in the state education system, Debra kept a busy schedule of meetings and conferences across the state. Her hours were long and her days full, but she tried never to permit her work to deprive her any more than necessary of being there for her husband, Kenneth, and their daughters, Kendrea and Kimberly. "Many of my Saturday mornings were spent at dance classes or gymnastics meets and my weekends traveling to cheerleading or volleyball competitions, as our daughters excelled at these sports. Now that both of them have graduated from college, finding that balance is a bit easier.

"Balance means also taking care of myself. For me to keep up my own can-do attitude, I need to take care of me. I take daily early morning walks with my husband or at home on the treadmill. I try to eat properly and make sure to drink lots of water. I find that when I feel better about how I feel and look, then my attitude, while it's normally positive, is even more positive. I read. I like to go to bookstores and get some Tom Clancy, but I also pick up self-help and religious books. I work on my spiritual, mental, and physical beings.

"One of the things I do in the morning is take five or ten minutes in prayer or meditation. Sometimes it's more prayer than meditation; sometimes it is just quiet time, thinking about things. In the summer it might be on a weekend morning when I can get up early and sit on our deck and just look at the trees in the back. I grew up an only child and I thoroughly enjoy my time alone. It was Kenneth, my childhood sweetheart, who helped me learn to share and to enjoy time with others as well. I intend to live until I'm eighty-five at least, and I'm over fifty now. [laughing] So I've got thirty some years to figure out what I'm going to do. And if I'm going to have the energy to do it, I need to pay attention to who I am as a person."

This sense of self and self-worth was instilled in Debra at an early age. It was a necessary component nurtured by parents raising their only child in Florida's segregated society and eager for her success. Both of Debra's parents were educators, graduates of historically Black institutions. "My father received his degree from Xavier University in New Orleans; my mother was a graduate of Florida A&M. Our family was the first Black family to live in Leesburg, Florida. I vividly remember 'colored' and 'White' signs on public restrooms and in doctors' offices. I attended segregated schools where the teachers were extremely supportive of their students. In high school all of us were expected to attend college, and they prepared us well for that transition. My family proudly encouraged my early leadership experiences as captain of the cheerleading squad and president of the church youth choir and other organizations. After integration I encountered some equally supportive White faculty and community members. I have been fortunate to experience affirmation and sponsorship/ mentorship from different races and genders."

Austin has over 30 years of experience in higher education. She has spent most of those years in Florida's community college system where she began as an English instructor at Lake Sumter Community College in the mid-1970s. She then rose through the ranks during 20 years of service to Tallahassee Community College (TCC), moving from assistant director of the Division of Applied Sciences to executive vice president, and, finally, serving as acting president for six months. The selection by the Board of Trustees of a sitting community college president from Texas to fill the permanent slot shocked the TCC community as well as the local African American constituency it served.

For Debra, one of the good things that came out of her failed bid for the presidency at TCC was the consistent positive acknowledgement of her character as a leader. "Even though the people I worked with didn't always agree with the decisions I made, they clearly believed that I had been fair, open, and communicative with them. And that was very important to me. I don't need people to always agree with me, but I do want them to know that I am honorable.

"My integrity permeates who I am as a person. Being credible, having a good reputation is critical to me, irrespective of my job. I want people to say Debra Austin is trustworthy, period. This is who I am. This is who I have always been. What has always been important to me is my name. I don't want my reputation sullied by anything that I have done.

"I don't think people last long when they lie, and the higher up you are in an organization, the more scrutinized you tend to be and the easier it is for people to catch you at lies. I don't want to lead like that. I can't. When people talk to me, they can trust me, trust that my word is my bond.

"When I hire people I ask, 'I know you're competent; what else do you bring to the table? What about your word? Am I going to hire you and hear people say, 'I can't believe she hired that liar?' Do you have integrity? What's your reputation? Are you a good team player? Or are you such an individualist that you can't get on with a team?

"I don't need a football team with all quarterbacks. I need a quarterback and a fullback and a wide receiver, and they all need to do their jobs so that together we can win. I get a little edgy when I sense that there is this 'I'm better than this person' attitude in the room. I try to model the behavior I expect from others. For example, if I heard our main phone line ringing and no one picked it up, I would pick it up. And I'd say to others, 'If I do it,

I expect you to do it. Just because it's not your job to be the receptionist doesn't mean that you can't pick up the phone and say, Chancellor's Office.'

"In any leadership role that I've taken, I've talked with a lot of different people in the organization. And I don't mean bringing them into my office and sitting them at my desk. I mean stopping by their offices or talking to them in the elevator or in the restroom. I've seen people walk into a restroom and not even acknowledge that there is a custodian in there by saying hello. That behavior really irritates me. The custodian works for the organization and is contributing to that organization. Anybody who works for an organization needs to acknowledge other team members.

"Now, I'm not a big fan of retreats for retreats' sake. But sometimes it's useful to get away from the busyness of the office and focus on an issue. Part of it is focusing on building team relations, getting people to interact with each other outside of the office, but still within a business context. Retreats let me learn about people's backgrounds and experiences because I listen. For example, one of the guys on staff in the chancellor's office is an accomplished pianist. He writes music and musical plays and is a music reviewer for the local newspaper. Just in passing, I said, 'I play the piano. It would be nice to see some of your music sometime.' He actually gave me an original score of a play that he was writing and a note saying, 'Thank you for being interested in my work.' I wrote back, 'Thank you for sending this to me. I'll attempt to play it, but I think it's far more advanced than my musical skills are.' When I saw him later and I told him I tried, but that I needed more time, we had a nice chuckle about it. My point is that I would never have known that about this gentleman had we not had the retreat and had I not listened. I probably go for weeks and never see him. But it was important for me to know, and he valued the fact that I showed an interest in his work. I see people as more than just blocks on an organizational chart.

"A leader needs to have people around her who know enough about various parts of the organization to make her successful. I believe very strongly in having extremely competent people working with and for me. Competence comes from books, experience, and from intuition. What I have found over the twenty-some-odd years that I've been an administrator is that I have good instincts. Some of that developed from becoming more confident in my decision-making capacity and abilities. I do know that if I get into a new situation I need to do the research and find out as much as I can about the organization or about the field. But at some point I say, 'I've learned enough to be comfortable with making some judgments about this particular area.' A leader doesn't need to know everything about the organization. Each of us brings something unique to an organization. We have different backgrounds, experiences, and ideas. Leaders must be able to bring all of that to bear as they make decisions.

"I believe in diversity of thought. When I am in a leadership position, I want a cross-section of people working together. I like people around who are positive-thinking people. I don't like negative energy. I want can-do folks who are well informed. I do a lot of information sharing (cross-informing) so that if one person is out, the whole unit doesn't come to a grinding halt because that person had all of the information. If a person hoards information, he or she holds us hostage. It might make that person feel good; it's power for him or her, but it is not good for the organization. If I asked the person who's over accountability, what's going on in strategic planning, I didn't expect him to know all the details, but I didn't expect him to say, 'I have no idea,' either. One has to be competent. Some individuals get by for a very short period on charisma and charm. They are usually great communicators, and they can mobilize people, but there is no substance.

"There are, however, a lot of competent people out there who just can't get their foot in the door. A sponsor helps you do that. A sponsor is someone who brings a protégé 'inside' by introducing her to people of influence, vouching for her ability and her integrity, and recommending her for special projects and important assignments. A well-placed sponsor facilitates career advancement. Sponsorship has been a key force in my career, but sponsorship can only take you so far. Competence has to show through."

One of Austin's ardent career sponsors has been T. K. Wetherell, who was in the Florida House of Representatives for 12 years, chairing both the powerful appropriations and higher education committees and serving as speaker of the House for 2 years. In 1995, he became president of Tallahassee Community College, which he led until 2001. In 2003, he took over the presidency at Florida State University (FSU). At TCC, Wetherell recognized Austin's organizational talents and promoted her to vice president. "He wanted me to replace him when he left TCC. When the Board of Trustees selected another candidate for the TCC position, I returned to my alma mater as assistant vice president of institutional effectiveness. And, when the position of chancellor of the State University System of Florida became available, T. K.'s influence certainly got my name on the list of candidates."

In 2001, the Florida legislature passed legislation (SB 1162), restructuring the entire educational system and eliminating the influential Florida Board of Regents that had controlled the operations of Florida's public universities for many years. This move proved controversial and was challenged and changed through constitutional amendment and has led to multiple, still-unresolved legal suits. As Debra assumed the once powerful and high-profile role of chancellor, the recently created Board of Governors was sorting out its role in providing direction for Florida's public universities. In addition, the universities were attempting to find their fit in the new system and to adjust to having their own boards of trustees.

"My job was to help the new Board define itself, while also determining the role of chancellor in this restructured system. Leading starts with vision: Here's what we want to do. As the leader I need to understand how to get there, but I'm not so focused on step one that I lose sight of where I want to be at the end of the day. My staff pays attention to step one; I've already moved on to three or four because I've got to lead them. It's almost like scouting," she laughs. "The scout goes out, surveys the landscape, and says 'Come on, folks, let's go here.' Then the scout goes farther, and these folks haven't even made camp, but that's the role. I know that I am already four steps ahead, so I need my staff to be taking care of the here-and-now.

"I'm comfortable with that arrangement because I hire good people, they know what my weaknesses are, and they fill in the gaps. I've had staff tell me that I have too many ideas and I'm not giving them enough time to work on 'step one.' I get impatient sometimes because we're not ready to move on to step two. I'm not the cheerleader type, but in some cases I need to be supportive and say, 'I know you can get it done.' In others, if they push back a bit, and I know that they are can-do people who are realistic, I'm more inclined to reevaluate whether or not *I'm* being realistic. The outcome of that kind of exchange depends on what the issue is. If it is an issue that I can back off of without compromising where I want us to be, then I might do it. But, if I can't back off, then I say, 'Do the best you can. It's not going to be perfect. We are likely to make mistakes or need to make changes, but that's why our pencils have erasers. Tell me where the weak spots are. Tell me where the potholes are. It's part of my job to navigate through them.'

"I am most proud of the fact that during the time I was in the chancellor's office, we collectively, the Board, the staff, and I, developed a strategic plan for Florida's higher education system. Although somewhat controversial and not universally well received, it did outline what we wanted our system to look like in the year 2012." When she left the office in 2005 to take a job at Florida A&M University (FAMU), Austin noted that, even with a plan in place, the challenges she began with still remained.

"Being on a campus allows individuals to really see the results of their work faster than when you work at the state level because you are closer to the action. That was appealing to me. Being at FAMU at the time that I was asked to go there was even more appealing because the institution itself was in a state of turmoil. It had had three different CEOs in three years and had been unable to establish and maintain adequate financial record-keeping procedures, which put the institution at the mercy of public and political scrutiny. I felt that my statewide experiences, plus other experiences, would be helpful to an institution in transition."

In the summer of 2005, FAMU Interim President Castell Bryant appointed Debra vice president for academic affairs and provost. Although Bryant had been president for less than a year, she had already rocked the institution through a series of major personnel and procedure changes intended to put FAMU on a new and more stable course. In the process, she had "fired more than 40 employees, frozen budgets, banned travel, and ordered payroll audits" (*Tallahassee Democrat*, August 18, 2005). Austin's appointment immediately generated more controversy as faculty leaders publicly protested the lack of faculty involvement in hiring the institution's chief academic officer. In addition, rumors abounded that her move to FAMU was the first step in a bid to become the institution's next president. "I did not attempt to address how I got there. I was there to do a job, and I knew I could do a good one."

Although she made every effort to communicate that she was not interested in a long-term commitment to the institution, her first address to the faculty as vice president included a long-range vision of the university from an academic perspective. This heightened suspicion in some faculty regarding her intentions about the presidency. She countered, "Whether or not Debra Austin is here, these are the issues that whoever is here will have to address. You as faculty need to keep these issues in front of whoever is in place. This is not my agenda, but the institution's."

Austin typically gets straight to the point. With two degrees in English, a bachelor's degree from Michigan State and a master's degree from the University of Florida, she expresses herself precisely with words chosen carefully. She uses a variety of formats to convey information. "Verbal, obviously, but written as well. I know when to be short and succinct in my messages and when to elaborate. If I'm meeting with someone who is very task- or goal-oriented, and we've got fifteen minutes, I don't spend time talking about their children or what they did last weekend. For other people, particularly women, there tends to be more of a 'let's talk about feelings, or how are you, let's be polite' expectation. It doesn't mean that a leader is schizophrenic; it's just [laughing] being aware of these differences and adapting to them.

"I also know how to craft communication for different purposes. I think to myself, 'Am I going to persuade you or convince you of something? Or is it that I really do want your input? So let's just talk back and forth. Or do I need to tell you 'no' in a way that you will best accept it?

"I tend to be very task-oriented. If a group looks at my five-item agenda and then starts talking about something else, I know that I need to back off a little bit because they want more of a dialogue than I have allowed for. Body language can also tell me a lot, and sometimes it signals: slow down. Effective leaders adapt. We have a wide variety of techniques and skills. What works in one situation or organization doesn't necessarily work in another. When you try to force it, staff are unhappy, and you become unhappy. If, in adapting, leaders are not comfortable, then they probably aren't going to be effective in the long run. The goals of the organization aren't going to be met, and it's just not a good fit."

She admits, "Internal communication at FAMU could have been enhanced all around." The FAMU School of Business & Industry (SBI) had been functioning without a dean since 2003. Shortly after arriving, Debra became embroiled in contract termination of eight professors that the president had mandated as part of the administration's accreditation plan for the unit. "There were goals for the SBI to become accredited. The faculty and administration had been working on it for some time. There unfortunately was not unanimous agreement on how to accomplish the task.

"I think the SBI had developed such an outstanding reputation that any attempt to make changes there would have been met with resistance, even changes that, internally, people knew were necessary. You don't have to have unanimity, but it is helpful to have a large consensus of people who will stand up and say, 'Yes, these are the kinds of changes we need to make if we are going to enhance our opportunities to become accredited.' And we didn't." The faculty members were given only a month's notice of termination, in conflict with institutional custom and termination guidelines in the university's union-negotiated faculty contract. Representatives of both the FAMU Board of Trustees and the faculty union registered protests over the firings. The chairwoman of the Board of Trustees called an emergency meeting to discuss the issue and later requested that the administration reconsider the firings. The firings became a galvanizing event for individuals who did not like other changes that were afoot for the SBI.

"Institutional change is more difficult than I ever imagined it would be. Changing the top leader and leadership team is really not enough to ensure institutional change. You have to bring people along. FAMU did not have the luxury of time to make the needed institutional/organization changes that *do* take time. There were pressures from the outside that did not permit them to have that time."

Debra Austin has held leadership positions at every level of higher education—community college, university, and state policy. She believes in the renewing benefits of change, not only for organizations but for herself as well. She has consistently found that at about three years she begins to look for a change in her career—for new challenges. As she puts it, "If the cure for some horrible disease was depending on me, we might as well hang it up. That kind of task requires a long-term commitment with multiple failures and minute gains that inch you toward a solution. I need to see more progress than that to get a sense of fulfillment. I know one way, and that is full steam ahead. My nature, my personality is: 'Let's get the job done' and move on to other things. I operate based on a predisposition toward action, and that action helps me stay committed. As the leader you have to be committed to what you do. If the leader is not enthusiastic about the goals and/or vision of the organization, it is virtually impossible to be effective because the people in the organization look to that leader for guidance, support, and motivation, all those things that make people want to follow. When I am in a leadership position, I convey enthusiasm and passion to employees by how I interact with them. I tell staff that within these doors I expect them to be open and honest. I expect us to have disagreements. I expect them to bring their ideas to the table. I want to foster creativity. I want to give people an opportunity to contribute, grow, and blossom. I want them to know that they are the experts. They can take chances, they can take risks, they can talk about things, and, I hope, feel good about the organization and themselves, and be passionate and enthusiastic about it. I try hard to show all people in the organization that their efforts are appreciated. Support people are extremely vital and valuable to any team effort. Because many of them operate behind the scenes, I make a special effort, use mental ticklers to remind myself, to send little notes that say, 'Good job, appreciate your team effort.'

"My advice to aspiring higher education leaders: Understand the education culture, know your strengths and weaknesses, be realistic in your assessment of your strengths and weaknesses and your expectations. Be willing and able to take risks and to be comfortable with the outcome of any decision that you make. Enjoy life—enjoy work—you spend a great deal of time there. Pace yourself. You won't be president overnight. Take a look at the job over the long haul, over months and years. Understand what will make you happy and satisfied in your career and go for it.

"It's about being self-aware. Effective leaders continually take stock of who they are, where they are going, what they have done, and what kind of vision they want to set for the organization. They are introspective. Over time they develop and get to know themselves. They monitor the environment in such a way that they're also monitoring their own behaviors. In so doing they are able to make changes based on that environment. It's good to reflect, but I don't spend all my time thinking backward. If I'm going to lead a team or organization, I doggone sure better know where we're going. Otherwise I'll lead them in circles, and that's frustrating for people and unproductive for the organization.

"There are things that we should do in a community because they are the right things to do. I think we have an obligation to do some things just with the aim of helping our communities, whatever those communities happen to be. I have always believed that through leadership I can help, I can make a contribution, I am making contributions to this world. And that makes me feel good. But, I also try not to take myself too seriously. People sometimes forget that they are not synonymous with the organization. I know that once I leave this world, the world's not going to end. And I'm okay with that."

BIBLIOGRAPHICAL NOTE

Debra Austin's chapter was written from information gathered from several in-depth interviews, informal conversations, her curriculum vita, and articles from the *Tallahassee Democrat* newspaper.

three

WALKING THE TALK

Lois Carson
Anneli Adams

W HEN I LEFT LOIS CARSON'S OFFICE and drove back home, I thought about the difference between nature and nurture. Natural ability or acquired competence? How do we know whether a person was born to lead, or whether her upbringing makes her who she is? Lois clearly makes a connection among her background, upbringing, and how she has developed through her life experiences. Twelve awards and multiple photos on her office wall reveal parts of her life. Five of the awards are Congressional. Most of the photographs show Lois in Washington, D.C. with other national education and political leaders who have made an impact in developing access, education, equity, and social justice in the nation.

Today, in her 70s, Lois leads a county agency with 38 employees, works full time to promote the importance of education and fight poverty, and has a hard time thinking of retirement. "My staff tells me that I am still the teacher with more to teach. My children wonder when I plan to slow down. But I have no plans for that. I agree with my staff; I have more to teach. I've been a career woman for most of my life. I have found great satisfaction in staying busy with six children, grandchildren, multiple jobs, and my community activities at local and national levels. In 2007, I lost my husband of fifty-five years. Now that he is no longer here, why should I stay home?

"I grew up in a very segregated south, in Memphis, Tennessee. Everything was segregated: schools, buses, restrooms, theaters, and drinking fountains. I was one of seven children, the only one to complete college and the only one to practice leadership at such a visible level. My father had only five years of formal schooling, but he always had a job; he bought two homes over his lifetime, and at his death left a financial legacy to his 25 grandchildren. He always believed that work did not give us dignity; rather we give dignity to the work that we do. He worked as a janitor, truck driver, and poultry farmer. He espoused fiscal prudence at all times and care of possessions. He illustrated his beliefs through such sayings as, 'Take care of your car and it will take care of you.' My mother went as far as the 11th grade, and at age 50 returned to school and earned her high school diploma. She was so smart, we never questioned her schooling, and she never told us that she hadn't finished high school. She was a visionary person who always made sure that there were reading materials around. Her motto: 'Feed the mind as well as body.' She stressed going to college, even though she did not know where the money would come from. We had to figure that out.

"Although our family had modest material means, my parents always encouraged us. They shared the vision that each of their children was going to be somebody. My dad used to say: 'Remember, naked to the world and you are somebody.' It was his way of saying that each of us had the potential to become anything we wanted in life. My mother also had grandiose goals for all of her children. She continually noted, 'I am preparing you to sit down with princes and paupers.' The first time I walked into the White House, her words made sense.

"I attended an all-Black Catholic school that was run by nuns. They were my first interaction with White people. The nuns prepared me for many challenges that I encountered later in life as a Black female leader. I regard those years as formative; they groomed me for life. They shaped me as a leader. In a Catholic school, you learn a lot of values. And, even though they were couched in religious terms, they were values of responsibility and commitment. Once I make a commitment, I do what it takes to get things done. I learned to stretch my vision beyond my grasp—to do more than I thought I could. The nuns were supportive of my talents and intelligence.

"They were certainly in cahoots with our parents. They said that they had three violins and that they thought I could learn to play." Lois laughs, "Did anybody ask Lois? My parents agreed, 'Oh, yes, she can learn to play a violin.' So, when I was told that I had to play a violin, I did it. We also had a piano. My great aunt played, my mother played, and I played. My friend Anita and I sang at my mother's club meetings. I have sung all my life in many choirs. Now, when I look back at these experiences I know I learned all the finer things as well as about following through on a commitment."

Lois was a good student and valedictorian of her class of 28 students. "I worked as a teacher's aide with little kids—first, second, and third graders. It was another way to hone my leadership and organizational skills. In my early teens, I founded a club of young girls and gave it a name, the Naïveté Debs. In high school, I was a cheerleader and served on the student council. One of the nuns noticed my activities and commented, 'You know, you have leadership skills. It's a gift from God, and you have to use them.'

"My future was determined early on. The nuns discussed it with my mother who told me, 'You are going to college.' I remember, in the 11th grade, asking one of the nuns what it takes to go to college and whether it cost money. When she answered 'Yes, it takes money,' I wondered, 'How can I go to college? I work every summer as a domestic and laundry worker and give half of my earnings to help the family meet household expenses.' But, the nun knew. She said, 'You can probably win a scholarship.' It was the close relationship between the nuns and my parents that put me on the path to further education." Lois won a United Negro College Fund scholarship and today holds a bachelor's degree and two master's degrees and is a distinguished alumna of both California State University and the University of California, Riverside.

"My mother was an active organization woman who belonged to many clubs. I emulated what I saw. I am so grateful to her for her vision of what I could be and the example she set for me. As a result, I love to work with younger women, to be a role model, to help them, to give back. Just last night, I was at one of my organizational groups doing leadership training." She laughs, "I always say that I am a groupie. I think you get more done in a group. I am a member of organizations for that reason. Over the years, I helped found the San Bernardino Commission on the Status of Women, the Inland Empire Chapter of the National Council of Negro Women, and the Diocesan Assembly for African-American Catholics."

Lois is a teacher at heart. "I love the written word, the spoken word. I love to write. I love to read. I care about others. I promote social change. I guess today I would call it being a leader." An English major, Lois worked at the University of California at Riverside in the 1970s where she taught composition at the School of Education. In addition, she directed Project Upward Bound, a program that helps low-income high achievers pursue higher education degrees. Because of her strong commitment to fairness for all people, she ultimately became a change agent with a calling and passion for changing conditions for people in need.

Lois is the first African American to be elected to the San Bernardino Community College District Board, where she served for over 24 years. Her commitment to social justice, which revealed itself as she helped develop the California community college system, is aligned with her belief system—a system that emphasizes continuous improvement of access and opportunities through education for representatives of underrepresented populations. For instance, during her tenure at the District Board, she led a fight to open child care centers on the district's two campuses to make it easier for working mothers to pursue higher education. "It was difficult to do with a board of six males who did not understand that the world had changed and that women were going to attend college and go to work, and that they needed child care. It was an economic necessity."

Besides her commitment to higher education in her district, she also served for seven years at the national level, on the Board of the Association of Community College Trustees (ACCT). ACCT recognized Lois in 1991 as the top trustee in the United States with the prestigious M. Dale Ensign Award for her exceptional contributions in higher education. The ACCT Board of Directors grants this award annually and honors an individual who has made a significant contribution as a lay trustee toward promoting the community college concept. "I served on the Board of Directors of the Association of Community College Trustees, where three major achievements resulted from my advocacy and probably led to the Top Trustee award. First, I raised the issue of low minority transfer rates from 2-year to 4-year colleges and provided a compelling argument for a strategy to improve the situation; the result was the Minority Transfer Program. Aimed at Black and brown students, it guaranteed that these students would gain formal, institutional orientation at both the sending and receiving schools. I also helped initiate the Dr. Charles Kennedy Equity Award, which recognizes community colleges that have strong diversity programs. Dr. Kennedy was the first Black community college trustee in the United States, and this award continued his memory while promoting a worthwhile objective. Finally, I urged the Association, which included Canadian 2-year colleges as members, to offer membership to Caribbean colleges as well. We also looked at how we could export the 2-year vocational college to third world countries.

"Along the way, my husband and I raised six children. The best decision I ever made was leaving work in 1955 and going home to raise children for about 10 years. I think that really made a difference. We had no money, but my dad had taught me the value of frugality with money and money management. He said, 'If someone gives you two pennies, save the first one and think about how you are going to spend the other one.' I have been a saver ever since. I had worked for the U.S. Air Force as a computer operator at Wright-Patterson Air Force Base in Ohio and at Norton Air Force Base in California while my husband was overseas. When he came home from the Korean War, we had enough money saved to buy our first house at the ages of 22 and 24. I often tell people that I was mending pajamas and making my own jam and we didn't have air conditioning, but I never thought of myself as poor until President Kennedy came on TV and said, 'If you are a family of this size and your income is such and such.' I said, 'We're poor. I need to go to work.' I took a temporary job and returned to college in 1964 to get my degree in English and secondary teaching credentials.

"I believe that I was born to do what I have done most of my life—that is to educate people and lead social change to improve the conditions for others. I first sought an elected position after I worked on John F. Kennedy's campaign. I really liked making things happen, working for a cause, and being committed to something. When I commit, it's because my conviction runs deep. I believe in doing what I believe is right.

"When my son was attending college, the college science department made a decision not to grant tenure to an African American professor, and the board of trustees did not question the decision. My son's friend asked: 'Mrs. C, what would you do?' I responded, 'Well, you need to get the education code and see if they followed the rules.' I got the code for the young men, went through it, and identified the right provision. We found that they had not gone through the process correctly. So I instructed the young people on what to do and how to help the teacher. I said: 'You need to act on his behalf. The only thing he needs to do is agree to a public hearing because you want to expose what happened.' They took it to the Board of Trustees. The trustees had to back down and the gentleman got tenure. As a result, the young people encouraged me to run for the board, which I did. The first time I ran I did not win, but the second time around I decided to read the state's master plan for higher education and nobody else on the campaign trail had read it but me. I was shining all over the place. It became very clear that I was going to win because I had done my homework. And, once I won, I contributed to *Trustees' Rights and Responsibilities*, published in 1997 by the Community College League of California. It outlined fair tenure procedures, among other things.

"My dad used to say, 'Mr. Opportunity only knocks once and you better know him when he knocks.' About 10 years ago I went to him and said, 'You know, Dad, Mr. Opportunity knocks more than once. In fact, sometimes you can make him knock.' I have learned that over the years. You can create opportunity."

During her years of service, Lois has had many opportunities. "I've been to Africa, Asia, South America, and Europe. I have been to Africa nine times. When we were in Togo, a little country in West Africa, we visited a northern village where the people speak a language called Ewe. A young girl there who spoke French, Togolese, Ewe, and English was our translator. I asked my group, our delegation, 'And, who is ignorant around here?' It was really eye-opening to travel the world with a mission of promoting higher education and at times discover that we, too, as a nation have much to learn about other countries. For example, in Africa, women learn entrepreneurism from childhood. They sell articles from trays on their heads, then progress to using carts, then stalls in the marketplace, and finally shops. They become astute businesswomen in the process. In Europe, I met women who carried out major leadership roles as a part of a long-standing tradition. During my trips to Finland, for instance, I came to realize that Finnish women represent the highest level of leadership across the society. They were, and continue to serve as, ministers, legislators, entrepreneurs, and scientists. Their current president is a woman who has been elected to her position twice."

Lois's leadership is guided by her ethics. "I really believe in honesty, fairness, equity, and follow-through. I respect others, and I think that you only get back respect if you give it. People can see through what you say and do if it is a facade. You can't demand respect; you earn it. Setting an example is important. I believe that I should practice what I preach and model the behavior that I want from other people. I do not believe in asking my staff to do anything that I am not willing to do. If things go well, I lavish praise on everybody. When things go badly, I accept the responsibility. I know that those around me are mature enough to recognize what I should assume as my responsibility and what I do not need to, but as the leader I accept it all. Walk the talk; I do believe in that.

"I'm a visionary person and I am creative. I have a lot of ideas. Ideas to me are like grapes on a vine. I have so many, some of them fall by the wayside. I am always coming up with them." She laughs, "My staff says I am headed in the front door, and some people are just coming in the back door, meaning I am always thinking two or three steps ahead of most everybody else."

In 2005, Lois's organization, the Riverside County Department of Community Action, was the first public, community action program to receive a national award of excellence. "One element of our vision is to find new solutions to old problems; hence, we are a 'creative ideas factory.' Two unprecedented ideas that we put into action illustrate what I mean. The Southeast Asian Peoples Farm Project was a response to an emerging population in the county who had all been farmers in their old country. We obtained two acres of donated land where they grow Asian and American produce to feed their families as well as sell at the marketplace. We got the University of California Agricultural Extension Program to provide training and technical assistance in sampling the soil and dealing with indigenous pests at no charge. We got the U.S. Department of Agriculture's local office to teach the farmers irrigation techniques. Today, there are seven farms and ancillary components, such as nutrition and English-language classes. This project touches the hearts of all who encounter it; it is the project people love to love!

"Similarly, when Congress passed the Temporary Assistance for Needy Families [TANF] Act, welfare reform legislation, in 1996, it was apparent that the result might be moving people off welfare but not out of poverty. So we looked for strategies aimed at those participants who could not find work and were hard to place. We recruited, trained, and deployed 50 TANF participants to survey over four thousand households, going door to door in the communities where they lived. They sought information on the status of each household, but also provided information about how to meet some of the needs revealed by the respondents. The experience transformed participants, mostly women who were coached on how to conduct job searches and then tracked for one year. We had a 70 percent success [rate] in job acquisition in permanent or long-term temporary employment. The model can be replicated anywhere since TANF is a national program."

These programs are a result of Lois's ideas, actions, leadership, and commitment to the betterment of life for all. But her leadership has not come easily, and she has been tested along the way. "I've been a trailblazer in many situations. You get your knees scarred when you are the first one down those trails. For example, I wanted to help a community group build a child care center and I wanted it to be a community operation as opposed to being run by a government agency. I helped the group get organized. We did needs assessments, and we started to work on getting things going. I went to the county council to talk about the organization and building a child care facility. We had the commitment of many local volunteers. A county council's representative berated me for putting the county in jeopardy by working with all these volunteers who had no liability. It really upset me, but I maintained my dignity while I was sitting there looking at him. When I got back to my office, I took my anger out on the door. Then I went back, and I continued to pressure and pursue him until he realized I wasn't going to give up. I demanded that he treat those people with respect. There have been numerous situations like that. I have a term for it: I just turn my lemons into lemonade."

Lois's perseverance has been acknowledged through numerous awards she has received for promoting social justice, including Leaders of Distinction Award, Lifetime Achievement Award, and Ann Kagie Award from the National Association of State Community Service Programs. In 2004, she received the Champions for Justice Award, given to people who have contributed to change by making personal sacrifices to advance positive social change in the world of the poor, senior citizens, the disabled, the homeless, youth, minorities, and others.

Time and time again, she models the behavior that garnered her these awards. "Being a role model is critical. In my life, it started with my parents and others close to me. My mother was my role model who showed me how to raise children. She was also a seamstress and sewed for a woman who was a teacher. That woman was everything I thought I wanted to be. I patterned my whole life after hers. Then, there were teachers in college and other adults. Today, the person I most often cite as someone who really impacted my life is Dorothy Height, the chair of the National Council of Negro Women. Dr. Height was the impetus behind my political and national leadership. I look up to her because she stands for integrity, honesty, commitment, and a vision for a better world, including equality and human rights for all people. There has always been somebody. My background and my upbringing made me the leader that I am."

Lois's advice to women who aspire to leadership: "Define the next step and know where you are going. Whether you talk about taking steps or going through doors, to be successful you must know where you are going. Always think of the next door that you are going through or the next step you are taking; name it and frame it so that it becomes real to you. You have to have a vision. Not a little vision, not tiny visions, you have to have big dreams. Your reach should always outdistance your grasp. You might only grasp this much, but you can reach as high as your vision can take you. I think that we dream too small. We corral ourselves into spots when we should leave our vistas opened and limitless. Even so, we must define the pathway. We should know what it is we are trying to get to and what we want to be. That takes introspection, reflection, discernment, sitting down with yourself, learning to like yourself, learning to know yourself very well, and being comfortable with yourself.

"I don't like it when women allow challenges to slow them down. I think we women, ourselves, are our greatest challenge. First of all, the perception that we can't do something, or dwelling on barriers, holds us back. We get consumed by how much it is going to take. I have always looked at the situation and said, 'Now, what do I need to do to remove some of these barriers?' The first time I ran for public office, I lost, but I learned enough to know how to get started on the next campaign. There are some definite barriers. There are income barriers and policy barriers, which are usually arbitrary. There is a glass ceiling. However, they can all be overcome through persistence. I try to focus on what I can do as opposed to what I can't do. I follow the old adage: Fake it 'til ya make it. Once I make a commitment to a cause, I'll do what it takes to get the results. For example, my commitment to making higher education accessible to more minorities is what drove my decision to get elected to the Board of Trustees of California Community Colleges. And, more important, it was this commitment that kept me 'fighting the battles' that I had to, to support my cause during the twenty-year period that I served as a trustee. It was by no means easy, but every minute was worth it."

In August 2007, Lois Carson received the 2007 Lyndon Baines Johnson Human Services award from the National Community Action Partnership in honor of her efforts to help low-income families change their lives. In March 2008, she was recognized as the 2008 Woman of the Year by the California legislature for her pioneering work in education and helping lower-income families improve their lives. So, was Lois born to lead, or did she become a leader through her life experiences? We will probably never know. What clearly matters is that Lois continues to walk the talk. Simply put, she leads.

BIBLIOGRAPHICAL NOTE

Lois Carson's story resulted from in-depth interviews, e-mail correspondence, exchange of information via fax, and the following websites: *Cal State San Bernardino News, San Bernardino County Briefs, Black Voice News Online,* and the website of Assembly Member Wilmer Amina Carter, http://democrats.assembly.ca. gov/members/A62/.

AUTHOR BIOGRAPHY

Anneli Adams, Ph.D., is executive director for professional excellence and international development at the College of Southern Nevada in Las Vegas. She also teaches in the higher education program at the University of Nevada, Las Vegas.

four

FINDING PURPOSE THROUGH MEANINGFUL LEADERSHIP

Marvalene Hughes
Dillard University

IN THE WINTER OF 2007, the ceiling-to-floor windows of Mar-valene Hughes's office suite overlooked the broken and boarded windows of a nearby hotel and the roof of the Super-dome, an image that figured prominently in the tragic news sto-ries about the Hurricane named Katrina. It was Katrina that took Dillard's administration from its campus home to this pink gran-ite high-rise office building in New Orleans's Central Business District. It is Katrina that has shaped, and continues to shape, Hughes's leadership role at Dillard.

Marvalene Hughes had been president of California State Uni-versity, Stanislaus, before accepting the presidency of Dillard University. She was the first woman and the first person of color to serve in that role at Stanislaus. "I went to Stanislaus when I was 53 years old. I told them that I would stay for 5 years and maybe more, but I wasn't sure. At the end of the 10th year, I knew I was finished because I had set very definite benchmarks, and I was in the process of meeting the final one—building the last building of several such projects during my presidency. At my annual evaluation, when the board asked me to continue, I said, 'I think I will, but I need some time to think about it.' As I thought about it, I decided that 10 years of presidential leadership at one university was a period with which I felt comfortable. So I told them that I was ready to leave, but that I would accommodate their request for one last year.

"Stanislaus was predominantly White when I arrived on campus in 1994. I had a goal of diversifying the university and increasing its student population, as well as expanding its fundraising, capital planning, and enrollment management. By the time I left, it had all happened. We had become a registered Hispanic-serving university and significantly increased the number of African American and Asian students. To increase the African American population, the university needed to be closer to where they lived. I convinced the State of California to allow me to take possession of a 102-acre site with about 50 buildings that it was closing down. It was tough because we had to get approval from the state legislature. It was a long, uphill battle, but the legislature finally approved the site for the university. It gave us the space in the right location to serve the African American population in the area. I had to find a developer and partner who would repair and redesign the buildings and create a multiuse facility, because we did not need all of that space. The site became California State University, Stanislaus at Stockton. Today, it is one of the most innovative initiatives in higher education. It recently built a new public school on the site as well as a center to help prepare developmentally delayed children and adults for entry into higher education.

"Part of my decision to leave California State University, Stanislaus, was based on a concept I have about leadership. I believe that leaders should strive to remain effective and not stay in their positions too long. You should know when you are really on top, and that is the time to leave. I think it was shortly after getting the Stockton campus established that the California Senate nominated me for President of the Year. I was undeniably on top. And it was time to leave."

For Hughes, the decision to leave while at the top of her game was liberating. "I had no plans, but I knew that I had a year to think about what to do next. It was a wonderful feeling to know that I was phasing out. I wanted to be unaware of what I would do next. I was at a point in life where I could be selective. Possibilities surfaced that I turned down, withstanding the temptation to become involved with options that would take me somewhere that didn't seem compatible with my values. During this time I became aware that I wasn't giving back to the African American culture to the extent that I wanted because I had been moving in a mainstream direction at major research universities. I no longer wanted to accelerate as a leader. I wanted to give something back.

"That is part of what the Millennium Leadership Initiative is about. It was founded by a few African American presidents (I was one of them) because we observed that, on the national level, the number of minority presidents was stagnating and declining. We began meeting to define the problem just prior to 2000. That is why it is named the Millennium Leadership Initiative. We started out planning to train African American presidents, but we realized that would severely limit our focus, and exclusivity was not our philosophy anyway. So we decided we would focus on individuals in protected classes, but we would open it up for everyone."

The programs of the Millennium Leadership Initiative (MLI) are organized under the umbrella of the American Association of State Colleges and Universities (AASCU). According to the AASCU website, the MLI was originally conceived to ensure that the next generation of higher education leaders reflects America's diversity, and it provides a focused and rigorous leadership development program for senior-level administrators. MLI is supported through grants, participant registration, and dues paid by the approximately 50 member institutions. Participants apply and are admitted through a rigorous selection process administered by a presidential committee.

"MLI is managed by presidents. Once a year, we train about thirty to thirty-five people from the dean's level and up who are poised to be presidents. We have organized a very intensive week that focuses on issues relative to the presidency. Four of us originators do much of the training ourselves. I usually open the session and offer the history about what it means to be a part of the MLI. We use our considerable experience. We take them through every dimension of training that is imaginable and essential to the presidency, including intensive one-on-one interviews with media, practical financial skills that are necessary, political skills, relationships with boards, diversity, contracting, fundraising, lobbying, shared governance—the full spectrum of the presidency. I have yet to have a participant who did not say, 'I do not know if you realize how unique the Millennium Leadership Initiative is.' Like me and many others, they have been to every leadership institute in the nation—Harvard, Bryn Mawr, Wharton, and others. What those institutes do is totally different from what we do in the Millennium Leadership Initiative. It has been amazingly successful. Since 2000, forty-five of our participants have become presidents. The MLI helped me fulfill my desire to give back and 'pay it forward.'

"Coming to Dillard gave me another opportunity to act on that desire. When the search firm called me about Dillard, I came to

New Orleans for a visit and I realized it was for this job that I was searching." Dillard is one of the elite historically Black private institutions; it serves a predominantly female student body of 2,000 undergraduates, many of whom go on to graduate school. "Just walking around the campus, it was beautiful. I knew that this was meant to be the next stage in my life.

"After eleven years as president of a California State University, I decided to take on a new and exciting leadership challenge. CSU Stanislaus was in excellent condition, and it had been my pleasure to serve it. I now took on a very special pursuit—one of personal passion and extreme importance. I was attracted to this position solely because I owe much of my early training and inspiration to the instruction and close mentoring I received at Tuskegee University, where I received my bachelor's and master's degrees. I am extremely proud of my heritage and the legacy of excellence with which I was imbued during those years. It was now my opportunity to give back in the very best way that I knew how, by joining with the Board of Trustees, faculty, staff, administration, and alumni of Dillard University to positively transform the lives and dreams of Dillard's students, so they, too, can achieve their ambitions."

Marvalene Hughes became president of Dillard University on July 1, 2005. About two months later, on Monday, August 29, Hurricane Katrina also arrived in New Orleans. "We had been watching the storm for several days to see if it was going to bypass Florida and, if so, would it enter the Gulf? Friday night, I continued to watch the storm's progress. All of the evidence was that this was a really, really strong hurricane. I had scheduled a staff retreat for Saturday. My husband and I watched the storm path again Saturday morning before I left for the retreat.

"The retreat was at a wonderful, isolated location. But early in the meeting, I felt I needed to check on the storm again. The manager found me a television. I could see that this huge storm had moved into the Gulf of Mexico and seemed to be heading straight toward New Orleans. The danger it posed seemed unreal because the sun was shining and no wind was blowing, but I really value life and safety. So I rushed back to the staff and said, 'We need to get back to campus.' Once back on campus, we made a very quick decision to close the university and get the students out of the city.

"Students had only been on campus about a week and they had scattered around New Orleans, exploring and experiencing the cultural environment, especially the new students. Getting them back to campus was a formidable task. We decided to put out an S.O.S. to all of the radio and television stations asking them to announce that we were evacuating and closing the campus and that students had to be back on campus by noon. It worked; they rushed back. A lot of activity gets underway when hurricanes approach, but because we were at least a day ahead of the game, by Saturday afternoon we had contracted all the buses we needed to get the students out of the city, and we had made arrangements with Centenary College in Shreveport, Louisiana, to shelter them. I boarded each bus to speak to the students and waved them all goodbye by sundown on Saturday.

"As they drove toward Shreveport, my husband and I drove to my sister's home in west Alabama. We made the trip safely, but about the time we arrived, I received a call that one of the buses had caught fire. I was so afraid that students had been hurt. The staff assured me that everyone was fine, but that they had to summon another bus. Because I had ordered the drivers to travel as a convoy, it meant that all the buses were parked on the side of the road waiting for the replacement. Although we had some adults with them, I thought, 'This has all been too traumatic for the students. It is my duty to try to get to Shreveport to see how they are doing.' And that is what I did.

"The resilience of Dillard's students is amazing. I visited with them and I went to chapel with them in Shreveport. A couple of them were very tearful, but otherwise they took it all in stride. On Sunday afternoon/evening, on my way back to my sister's house, I was in the thick of the storm. Driving was terrible, but I felt better knowing that I had done what needed doing by showing care and concern for the students. I think that is really important in leadership generally—caring about your people, caring about students.

"After the storm passed, I returned to New Orleans to find more than four hundred million dollars in damages at Dillard's fifty-five-acre campus. Hurricane Katrina was not what caused the fiasco. What Katrina left was all of the damage from trees and roofs and such, but Katrina did not leave the eight to ten feet of water that ultimately flooded my campus.

"Dillard is located near the levees that broke and, as a result, incurred considerable damage. The campus was under water for several weeks. Three buildings burned down completely, including the dormitories. Several buildings at the back of the campus, on the lowest part of our property, could not be restored. Lawless Chapel is the only building that was not under water. We had more than two hundred members of a remediation team engaged in campus clean-up. Remediation meant going into every single building, determining the level of damage, drying the floors, and providing some ventilation to avoid mold, to protect against it, or to contain it. Then the buildings had to be assessed by architects and engineers to determine the possibility of restoration and reconstruction.

"My major concern was the people. I wondered if I knew how to protect and adequately care for a totally wounded community:

wounded students, many of whom had lost their jobs, and wounded faculty. The students who lived on campus had lost everything, of course. Many of those same students had also lost their family homes. A good number of the faculty had lost their homes as well. We had all those people who were in shock. I tried to do what was right for them." Although the university could truly not afford it, Dillard paid full salaries to all faculty and staff for the months of September and October. No other New Orleans university did that. "My personal losses were very minor, as I had not relocated my household possessions from California. But I had almost lost Dillard University, a campus with a one-hundred-thirty-six-year legacy of educational excellence."

In speaking with a reporter from the *Black Collegian* after Katrina, Hughes commented, "I learned that there is not a book that has been written and not a university in the nation that has had to completely restore itself as Dillard has; that I had to write the book. I had to determine step-by-step what needed to happen. I had to educate myself and lean on other people. I had to lean on the faculty to perform with the highest level of commitment to excellence. I had to lean on the students to believe in us. They leaned on me, and we leaned on each other through difficult times. What I learned is that a community under adverse circumstances can come together and transform itself."

On Monday, January 9, 2006, Dillard University reopened in the Hilton New Orleans Riverside Hotel. "The hotel staff worked around the clock throughout the holidays to prepare for the students' arrival. We were able to rehire about fifty percent of our faculty members to ensure that Dillard faculty taught Dillard students. About fifty percent of our two-thousand pre-Katrina students came back for the spring semester. It was encouraging, considering that we were not yet back on campus." The Hilton general manager set aside for Dillard more than 1,000 beds from among the 1,616 rooms, calling it "a win-win situation" that not only helped the university but also enabled the hotel to keep many of its workers on staff.

"When our students arrived in January, there were signs all over the hotel that read, 'Welcome to Dillard University.' The hotel staff did very special things to make us feel welcome." In honor of Dillard's mascot, they created the Blue Devil Cafe, a cafeteria section of the hotel's restaurant that served the Dillard students three meals a day. They set up a campus post office and a student-only laundry room. Students also had housekeeping twice a week; use of the hotel fitness facilities and business center, and a Wi-Fi Internet connection. "We were able to get comfortable living arrangements for our students at the Hilton Hotel, and they paid only what they would have paid had we been on campus." Classes were held in the hotel's ballrooms.

A part of bringing the Dillard community back together involved beginning the healing process. "My academic discipline is psychology. I felt great empathy for the faculty, staff, and students who lost so much. We made the traditional counseling programs available, but this was a unique situation, and we took additional steps. We engaged our students in a Katrina service project.[1] We also had open sessions where students were invited to share their perspectives and talk about what was happening to them. We made it possible for them to have flexibility in their activities. That said, the academic programs were more intense than usual because we decided to give them two semesters' worth of course work between January and July 1. That really tightened the calendar for them.

---

1. For many years, Dillard students have been required to complete at least 120 hours of volunteer service as a graduation requirement.

"As president, it was interesting living together with faculty, students, and staff in the hotel. I think doing so is why we realized how much we needed each other. When I had enough energy, I would come downstairs, sit in the cafeteria, and eat with students. Even though I had some very tearful moments with students who were so bonded to the campus and who feared that they might not be able to graduate from Dillard, I continue to be amazed by their tenacity and resilience. We were so determined and so emotionally committed. Because we had such resilience and tenacity, we persevered even in the most difficult times. I now know that if you do not have resilience and stamina, other things probably don't matter. I had difficulty understanding it at first. If I had time to do research, it would be on the resilience of our faculty, staff, and student population. It seems to be a New Orleans attitude, the attitude that we know how to bounce back.[2]

"As a leader, if you are not resilient, you can get bogged down with disappointment when something has not gone perfectly, and then you have difficulty bouncing back and getting beyond it. I devote a great deal of my time to not getting mired in setbacks, not getting dragged down by other peoples' negative agendas. There will always be those agendas swirling around in your environment, no matter where you are. If you get caught up in them, you can become them and begin to lose your own focus and your own identity. Physical and emotional stamina and energy undergird resilience. The amount of time required in the presidency is unpredictable, and the level of resources that must be expended is daunting. If you do not have stamina and energy, you simply cannot do your job.

---

2. And bounce back they did. On July 1, 2006, more than 350 Dillard seniors made the traditional march down the Rosa Freeman Keller Avenue of the Oaks to receive their degrees on the Dillard campus. And the following September, classes were again held in the beautiful white buildings graced by the ancient oak trees and spacious green lawns for which Dillard University is well known.

"For me, energy is not just physical or emotional, although both are terribly important. Spiritual energy is paramount. Spirituality is a crucial dimension that I would like to see developed more in leadership. I am not saying that it has to be Christianity. I happen to be a Christian, but I am saying that spirituality really needs to be developed so that there is passion and an awareness that there is a force that guides and protects you. That force tells you that you are not all alone as you lead an organization. Spirituality gives me a sense of security that nothing else can provide. Spirituality and security are important aspects of leadership.

"I am very mindful of paying attention to and experiencing my spiritual depth during the day. It is not something I plan or schedule, but there are just times when I am aware that I need to get out of the exclusively intellectual mode and move myself into a different space. When I can do that, I feel a unique sense of groundedness. I experience my spiritual energy especially when I encounter a tough activity and have difficulty getting through it. If I can take a deep breath and allow myself to know the power that is there and recognize that it is guiding me, it becomes easier. The presidency is quite demanding, and I know that more than my physical body is engaged in all this complex activity. There is something that guides me in the universe. And I try not to get in the way of it.

"Many people who know me believe I was meant to be here at Dillard at this time. I have received letters from people in California and other places suggesting that they wondered why, at that point in my life, I left California State University, Stanislaus. They wondered why I would choose Louisiana over California, but now they know. When Hurricane Katrina happened, they said, 'That is it.' I have begun to believe it as well. And it is in believing that I am able to recommit, to give my very best effort to moving the university forward. If, after all, this is my providential responsibility, I want to do it right. As I reflect on the amount of energy and personal effort devoted to leading this institution seven days a week, I realize that I have been guided by something much larger than I.

"In addition, there is something spiritual about being a member of the Dillard University family, and something so special about being the president of an HBCU [historically Black college and university] with a strong academic identity and standards of educational excellence. Working with people whose backgrounds are largely the same as your own is divine. There is a kind of personal bonding that is hard to describe. When I put my heart and my soul into something, I have to be passionate about it. It was that passion that gave me the extra adrenalin on which to operate during the crisis. My heart and my soul and everything about me consider this to be my life's mission. I had never thought of a life's mission until Katrina hit.

"If I am not passionate about what I am doing, I do not enjoy it, and I do not do it as well as I can or should. That is one of the reasons I have been selective recently. I have had some jobs for which I did not have a lot of passion. One of the jobs I had was just a geographical fantasy, not a good reason if you are interested in relocating for career advancement.

"I was in California the first time for fifteen years at San Diego State University. You do not leave San Diego, because it is so wonderful. You do not even think about leaving until you realize that nobody else is thinking about leaving, either. So this was not a glass ceiling; it was a cement ceiling. All my bosses were settled in their positions, and they decided to give me more responsibilities. So my portfolio grew broader and broader, and that was fun. Two or three times my title changed, but I was still doing basically the same job. Back then I looked at my career differently. I believed that if you were doing well and you were where you wanted to be, then there was no reason to relocate. So I had passion about the university and what I was doing, but frankly I had no career mobility.

"I finally moved from San Diego State University to Arizona State, where I became an associate vice president. It was that move that caused me to realize that I needed to be mobile if I wanted to move up in administration. From Arizona State, I allowed myself to be wooed to the University of Toledo by its president because I wanted to work with him. He was a remarkable person. I thought he was the ultimate—a gentle, warm person and a visionary leader. He was very clear and direct about what he wanted and really understood how to get people behind his agenda.

"When you think about it, most of a leader's time is devoted to communicating your messages and your motivation or leading by example, which is a way of communicating as well. In my roles as a leader, my profession has served me well. In administration and counseling you learn to understand human behavior in a different way. I know how to listen and articulate the issues that are most important, I know how to listen for feelings and content, pain, joy, and sorrow, and I know how to respond to those factors. I know how to be a nonjudgmental communicator. I use these skills every day of my life in everything I do. If you can listen, if you can motivate people, and if you can plan—well, that is what this business is all about. This is an interesting antithesis to believing that a university president has to be a physicist.

"When I went to Toledo to sign my contract, the president whom I looked forward to joining told me he was going to Virginia Tech. He said, 'I want you to know that I had not planned to do this, but this opportunity came along.' And then he said, 'You know, there is a position open at Virginia Tech and you just might want to pursue that' (which explained my unexpected calls from Virginia Tech, where it seems I had been nominated for a vice presidency, and they were eager to have me apply). I just looked at him and said, 'I just signed a contract. I will honor that contract. I am not following you farther. I came here because you convinced me that I wanted to be with an administrator like you. But now you have chosen to leave. I will find my way somehow.' I will never forget that moment, because it was really the point at which I came into and found my own strength as a leader.

"But, I had made the move for the wrong reason. I went because of his persuasive style and his personality, and I went because he gave me a list of exciting things to do. Give me a list and tell me it is going to take five years, and I will do it in two years," she laughs. "I had to learn how to operate in a new environment where the new president did not choose me. So I took on that list. I worked diligently on that 'to do' list, and he was very pleased with my work. But I think the bond had been broken when the person who recruited me left. I did not feel connected to the institution and I didn't stay very long."

Hughes's next position was vice president for student affairs, vice provost, and professor at the University of Minnesota. "I loved it there. I stayed at Minnesota for four happy years until I heard from California that they wanted to talk with me about returning as a president. Around that time, the president at Minnesota took my husband and me to brunch and told me, 'You know, you might want to consider applying for a presidency.' I was taken aback and I blurted out, 'What? Am I not doing my job well? Are you trying to tell me something?' He replied, 'Yes, I'm telling you you're ready for the next step.' His confidence in me helped me realize my own competence to run an institution.

"Being competent is essential. I am not at the stage where I do this now, but I used to deliberately reflect on what competency means in the academic community, and what one has to do to bridge from one role to the next. We work in an academic culture, and if you want to be successful, you must play by the rules of the game. In the academy, I was aware that I needed to do research; I needed to write and publish. I needed to be a scholar. For me, this was a confidence builder, a matter of knowing that my intelligence was recognized and proven, and my mental capacity was also considerable, if I applied myself.

"I think it is especially essential for an African American woman to be able to state, 'Here are my credentials,' knowing that they will compare well with all the others.' You have to prove your competence. And the expectation of your competence is not at the same level of expectations of the White female and male. Yours has to surpass both.

"Messages from our parents are very important in building confidence and a sense of competence. Particularly, I recall a message my parents taught me about being African American and realizing you must be twice as good, but, yes, you can do it. My wonderful parents produced nine successful children, because of the messages they gave us. All of us are college-educated; several have advanced degrees. Education was not an option. They never asked, 'Do you want to go to college?' It was truly a given. I really thought that college automatically came after high school, just as middle school follows elementary school.

"There are little tidbits that parents can drop. My mother was an elementary school educator. I will never forget something she told me. She said, 'Remember, when you go into a new position, ninety percent of your success is acting as if you are absolutely, totally prepared and in charge. So just remember, act as if, and it comes together. That is what White males do,' she said. 'They act as if they are the world's best person for that position, and the rest of us buy into it.'

"I think the opportunities are increasing and broadening for women in higher education and, to a lesser extent, the compensation is following. A few women presidents have outstanding salaries, but not like some of the men presidents and coaches who are making millions per year. I am optimistic that we are making progress. It is not as rapid as it should be, and it is not in all areas of the academy. Still, we have cracked the ceiling and we have more women presidents than we had in the past. Women in the Ivies and at major research universities are increasing as well.

"I advise women who want a career in higher education to get a good, solid education and decide what field really is the right fit for them. Once you get into your field, I believe it is important to understand the values and the qualities that enable you to move forward. Of course, at an academic institution, values that advance you include teaching, research, and service. It is important to develop a good track record in those areas, and then move into management positions if that's where you want to be. Build a foundation as you move forward so that you do not have any big gaps. I have seen people move up who had gaps in their understandings because they moved too fast. Gaps in your experience can affect your sense of confidence and the security that is necessary in a major position. Not having a true sense of confidence and competence as a leader can make you feel that, when somebody questions your actions or a decision you made, they are questioning your leadership. If you are confident that you are competent because you have had all the necessary experiences along the way, it is easier to be able to decide that it is okay to change your mind if you make a recommendation and there are indications that you need to reexamine it. A good foundation helps to develop your confidence and a true sense of competence as well as credibility.

"People who do not include establishing credibility on their leadership agenda are destined to have difficulty. You must understand the values and culture of the academy and at the same time remain true to your own values. You must establish your trustworthiness and bring integrity into your leadership. If you do not have integrity, if you do not have consistency between what you espouse and what you do, there will be major problems. If you do not have values that are consistent with the way you live, think, and act, the inauthenticity will be noted. Inauthenticity creates mistrust, a lack of credibility, and disbelief about everything that is being advanced. To have the kind of integrity that I am talking about, your sense of ethics must be very clear and you cannot equivocate. Even if I know that no one anywhere has the possibility of knowing or seeing what I am doing, I still want to be sure that what I am doing is right.

"We have all seen leaders whom we think have strong values and ethics but sometimes are on the wrong side because they become focused on the wrong goals: winning, earning a lot of money, getting a big promotion, and having a title. Those accomplishments become extremely important to them. Such selfish concerns can distract a leader from taking care of the organization.

"Integrity and consistency of values must be enacted because people always observe what the leader does. I was with a person this afternoon who talked about what she called my 'inclusivity and involvement.' Those are certainly concepts that I value. She said it was refreshing, 'You're accessible. I've watched you walk up and down the hallway. I have noticed that the custodian receives the same respect as the chairperson of the faculty council. If you meet a custodian, you stop and talk.' Once, in California, I was walking across campus with a very high-level policymaker. One of the gardeners was driving a lawnmower. I can still see his lovely, smiling face. I stopped and said hello. And he said, 'You know, that is something that we have always appreciated so much about you. You speak to us no matter where you are or who you are with. There are others who never even look at us.' I cannot imagine doing that.

"Values and ethics are learned at any early age by doing and observing. I grew up in a family that truly believed in respecting and valuing each individual, and I live that value every day. That is who I am. We all should have the values of goodness, morality, and humanity, especially leaders, and we should understand that everybody is good and equal. I have internalized that message, and I live by its premise.

"It will seem strange to people, but coming to Dillard University under these unpredicted circumstances was one of the best things that happened to me. I say that because I did not know myself before as clearly as I do now. I learned much about myself in my previous positions, but nothing parallels what I now know about myself. I would never have learned these things had I not come to Dillard. I had never been challenged as much as I am now. I truly did not realize the level of personal resources and energy that I had until I had to put every ounce of my existence behind the mission of restoring Dillard. A lot of things change in situations like the one we have faced here. What was enormously important to you in the past becomes the least important to you. Before this experience, I viewed myself as carrying out a career plan—moving up the ladder by doing all the right things to be able to advance. Now I see myself as having a mission and a purpose. Nothing is more noble than having a career that represents your life's purpose."

BIBLIOGRAPHICAL NOTE

This chapter is based on a compilation of material gathered from interview transcripts; articles from *The Black Collegian* October 2005; *The Black Collegian Online,* http://www.black-collegian .com; *New Orleans CityBusiness,* May 15, 2006; Dillard University website, http://www.dillard.edu; and American Association of State Colleges and Universities website, http://www.aascu.org/ mli/index.htm.

us to meet guys. I realized at that point that I had good organizational skills. So when I was in graduate school, I was involved in the civil rights movement and I worked with the Student Nonviolent Coordinating Committee to organize students. Later, as a graduate student, I also organized the female graduate students in the Anthropology Department at UC Riverside to protest the fact that male graduate students made more money than the females did. We also organized to get a course on the books, called 'Women in Cross-Cultural Perspectives.'"

Moses received her master's and doctorate degrees in anthropology and graduated with highest honors from the University of California, Riverside. She accepted a faculty position at California State Polytechnic University–Pomona (Cal Poly) after graduating and early in her career participated in the California Leadership Development Program. "I had the opportunity to go to Long Beach State and be an assistant in the dean's office for a year. At the end of that year, I decided I was going back to teaching because I didn't think that I wanted to be an administrator. But it was never the same. I had seen a university from a larger perspective than most of my faculty colleagues had, so I had a whole different view.

"I became the spokesperson for the department and spoke out on many occasions. Once the dean heard me and said, 'Well, if you think you can do this job so much better, then why don't you do it?' So I took on a leadership role at Cal Poly that really changed my direction. I took on a struggling women's studies program and a poorly attended ethnic studies program. The dean wanted something done with them, or he wanted to get rid of them. I went in and changed the many small programs into a coherent department, the Department of Ethnic and Women's Studies, one of the few in the United States in the early 1980s. We developed a curriculum that integrated issues of class, race, and gender. It was very progressive for its time. None of the small programs could have survived as separate majors, so we came up with one interdisciplinary major and a series of minors that complemented the polytechnic nature of the university. It became a very strong curriculum and department.

"I did that for two years, and then the dean of my college was fired and they were going to choose an interim dean from among the department chairs. The provost and the president asked me to do it. I have to give them credit for going out on a limb. Employees with more seniority than I had questioned the choice, but because I'd participated in that administrative training program, I was ready. I had the skills to do it, I had the reputation for getting things done, and I had the respect of my colleagues.

"I thought that the position of interim dean would be one year, and then I would return to the Anthropology Department. However, a delegation of faculty came to me, just as a national search for the position was getting started, and asked me to throw my hat in the ring. I was amazed, totally amazed, but again, the same values motivated me—how to make this a better place, how to be inclusive, how to have a sense of integrity, how to problem solve, how to herd cats basically. I said all right, and after a long process, I was chosen."

Moses was dean of the College of Letters, Arts, and Social Sciences (CLASS) at Cal Poly from 1982 to 1988. When she began, there were very few women department chairs as well as problems with a lack of multicultural curricula in many areas. "My whole goal was to create a more inclusive environment, to create an environment that honored and respected difference but built community around that difference. In general, we were talking a whole lot about access and diversity, but most institutions were not doing anything about it. At Poly, leadership didn't seem to know what to do. Even though CLASS was the largest college in the university, most of the majors were in the sciences. We worked to develop more liberal arts majors and to create a curriculum that spoke to students in the sciences and the professional schools. When I left, over half of the department chairs were women and minorities and the curriculum had changed.

"I was the only woman and the only African-American on the Council of Deans at Cal Poly. It was in doing that job that I realized that I could be president of a university. When I saw how presidents work, I saw how some of it was serendipity. I watched how they developed their leadership styles, and I thought, 'This isn't rocket science. I think I can do an even better job.' There were things that I would need to do to be prepared, but I could do them. At every level, search committees look for ways to screen people out, so I knew that I had to take all the administrative positions and training opportunities that I could that would lead up to the job of president."

In 1988, Moses went to California State University, Dominguez Hills, as vice president for academic affairs. Cal State Dominguez Hills was opened after the 1965 Watts race riots. "It was a unique and tough setting. We had students from South Central L.A., students from East L.A. All these students, and returning housewives from Palos Verdes, converged on the campus. It was like this nexus of race, class, and gender. If you were in the parking lot, you saw everything from jalopies to BMWs. The leadership of the campus didn't quite know how to harness such diversity.

"I immediately saw things we could start doing to create a university that valued inclusion, diversity, and excellence. For example, we instituted diversity hiring programs to improve the ethnic and gender mix of the faculty, and we talked about the importance of doing searches well. It wasn't until I started shutting down searches that people took me seriously. I told faculty members from the School of Business that they had to do a better job of bringing in a diverse pool of faculty. A couple of senior faculty didn't agree and responded with, 'We're not going to be on the search committee anymore.' I said, 'Fine, I'll constitute another one.' And when they saw that I was going to move ahead without them, they changed their minds and stayed on the search committee. I also worked to integrate the university and the community through programs that helped African American and Hispanic youth from South Central L.A. to stay in school and get jobs, and through initiatives that prepared gifted minority students in math and science for applications to high-ranking traditional and technical universities around the country.

"In 1991, when the second set of riots hit Los Angeles, our campus was used as a staging ground for the National Guard to go into L.A. It was poignant for me. From my office I could see plumes of smoke in different parts of the city. I discovered that, for the immigrants and refugee students who were coming into California from places like El Salvador and Guatemala, seeing an active military presence was harrowing. I found that the African American and Latino students had ambivalent feelings about the troops on campus, and that the White students were just happy that the police and National Guard were there to protect them. These three sets of students had three different realities and the question became: How do we turn this into a teaching moment?

"We closed down the university and had a teach-in where we heard all these different perspectives about what was going on from various groups of students and staff. My training in anthropology really came in handy when we were talking about cross-cultural differences and their implications for the community, the university, the faculty, and the students. The experience of this educational encounter opened the faculty's eyes because, for the first time, many of them saw who their students were as individuals. They had been looking at the students in a very homogenous kind of way. I think the experience helped create a kind of community among students and faculty that hadn't been there before. They saw how special they, and the place in which they were teaching and learning, were. We had embraced diversity in all of its complexity."

In 1993, Ann Reynolds, a friend, former chancellor of the California State University System, and new chancellor of the City University of New York "reached out" and let Moses, among others, know about the opening for president at the City College of New York (CCNY). On May 29, 1993, the *New York Times* characterized CCNY as an institution "inundated with students unprepared for college work and suffering from excruciating budget cuts, requiring tuition increases and loss of faculty and staff positions," all of which "hurt the institution's academic standing."

"CCNY had a wonderful history of being an opportunity university for smart, first-generation New Yorkers and for immigrants and children of immigrants, particularly Jewish kids who couldn't get into Harvard, Yale, or Princeton because of discriminatory practices. To date, twelve Nobel Laureates have come out of that institution. If I were ever to be president of a college or university that resonated with my values, this was the place. I wasn't looking for a presidency. I was looking for my next job and the right fit. And the two things just came along at the same time; that's the best way to describe the process. It chose me and I chose it. It was that kind of relationship."

At age 46, Moses came in as the institution's 10th president, and, although not the first African American, she was the first woman to hold that office. She was brought in to make deeper budget cuts, reorganize departments and programs, and repair the reputation of the institution. She also faced several unanticipated issues coming into the job. First, she was approved for the position by every one of the trustees except one, a fact that would come back to haunt her. Second, some of the more conservative media painted her as "the diversity queen of higher education," not a positive concept in New York in the 1990s. And, third, an earlier First Amendment rights controversy involving one of the institution's African American professors had yet to be resolved, a factor that increased criticism and apprehension about how Moses would support and promote diversity at CCNY. "I've always been guided by the principle that you have to do the right thing. If it's tough, well, so be it. It's going to be best for the institution in the long run to do the right thing. Otherwise, why do the job?"

In 1970, CCNY went from selective to open admissions. Although ended in the late 1990s, the practice resulted in a wider academic spectrum of students at the institution. Approximately one-half of the students entering CCNY in 1999 were foreign-born and many of them did not speak English at home. "The conflict was how to convince people who thought otherwise, that you can have an institution that's committed to racial and cultural diversity and have it be academically excellent at the same time. These were seen as two separate poles and I was trying to bring them together. People resisted. To complicate matters further, we had over ten different faculty, staff, and employee unions fighting for the same limited resources.

"The state had a budget shortfall, and it needed to figure out ways to close the gap. Cutting our budget was one of them. They had been making cuts over a period of years, but nobody looked at what the cumulative affect had been on the institution." On July 11, 1999, the *New York Times* reported that state appropriations had decreased 40% since 1980, and city appropriations had decreased by almost 90% during the same period.

"I had to close down programs, merge departments, and fire some faculty. That's what people remember. We also had an incident where the chief of police used monies for security cameras in an attempt to recover stolen computers. It was only a few thousand dollars, and it was done without my knowledge, but the students saw this move as an attack on them. Talk about three hundred sixty degrees. I got three hundred sixty. Faculty were mad at me. Students were mad at me. The city was mad at me. The government was mad at me. I met regularly with various union leaders, Academic Senate leaders, and external community and city leaders. My job was as much outside as it was inside."

Moses's vision for CCNY was to build on the founder's belief in access to quality higher education and to incorporate the needs of CCNY's students and the community in a plan that was relevant for the institution. During her presidency, several programs were created that met with outstanding success.

"I found that there was a perception in the community that CCNY did not address the needs of the surrounding Harlem area. It was in part because, before I arrived, the continuing education program was dissolved due to crippling budget cuts. The community wanted it reinstated. I began by asking, 'If we bring the program back, how do we bring it back so that it's relevant?' The president of Columbia and I came in as presidents of our respective institutions at the same time, and we didn't know that we weren't supposed to help, cooperate, and collaborate with each other. We just did it. Together, we worked with the federal government to create a federal empowerment zone that included the Harlem neighborhood. Graduate students from both institutions surveyed locals regarding the needs of the community, economic development, and infrastructure. The continuing education program was then designed and developed to address the needs delineated by the community.

"We also developed a student aid program to support our existing biomedical program. M.D. and Ph.D. students received loans to attend school and, after graduation, worked in the community for specified periods to pay off their loans. The community received much-needed medical care and the students were able to attend and afford graduate schooling.

"The publishing certificate program that we developed linked the university with all of the publishing houses in New York. Editors and associate editors taught the courses at CCNY and the students served in internships with the publishing companies. The benefits were mutual. The publishing industry appreciated the infusion of students with broad linguistic abilities and global backgrounds, and students gained valuable training and job opportunities and, in the process, grew professionally." This program recently celebrated its 10th anniversary and invited Moses back to attend the commemoration.

"We also set up an alumni program to offset tuition for low-income students. By the time I arrived in 1993, tuition at CCNY had climbed to over three thousand dollars per year, which was prohibitive for many of our students. I went to alumni whom I knew could afford the tuition and asked them to give back to CCNY what they had received—a free education. I explained to donors that, in current dollars, it would cost approximately twelve thousand dollars to fund four years of college for a poor student at CCNY. That is what I asked them for. The request resonated with people who could not or would not give millions of dollars to the university and it met with great success.

"Access, relevancy, and community: It's a model based on the needs of the community around the university that retains currency today. In my time at CCNY, the university became 'the catalyst' that brought the community, students, and organizations together. And it helped the students. Diversity is about the students changing, too. It's not just about other people relating to them. It's about their seeing the world in a different way. The vision I had is that everybody would use this educational opportunity to grow, wherever they were."

Although Moses experienced success as a president, the public environment was changing. "I probably should've read the tea leaves more in terms of the political changes that were taking place. Two incidents serve as examples. The first involved a gift to CCNY for a scholarship that would enable students to do community engagement work. As a condition of the donation, the donor wanted her picture taken with the mayor of New York and students in the program. The mayor, Rudolph Giuliani, refused. The one trustee who had not voted for my hire told him that CCNY was not a first-class institution, and that if he had his picture taken with the students and me, he would be showing that he supported the college. The donor was insulted and withdrew the funding.

"The second incident occurred near the end of my tenure as president. In 1998, I asked the First Lady of the United States, Hillary Clinton, to be the 1999 commencement speaker. In 1999, Clinton announced that she was going to run on the Democrat ticket for senator of New York. Rudolf Giuliani, then mayor of New York City, decided to run for the same position on the Republican ticket and through intermediaries asked me to 'uninvite' Clinton. I refused.

"In addition, one major problem was the board. Ten board members were appointed by the state and five were appointed by the mayor. The board that hired me had turned over completely in the seven years that I was at CCNY. The agenda for the institution went from providing an excellent education to an underserved populace to making CCNY into another Massachusetts Institute of Technology [MIT]. The board wanted us to raise our admission SATs and to focus on science and engineering and forget about everything else. It was the board's new vision of excellence for the university and a change in mission and direction for the institution.

"Other changes also occurred. The university and its mission were under attack by the conservative Republican administration. I had come in under a Democratic governor and a Democratic mayor. The one trustee who had not supported my candidacy for this job became chair of the board and then used the university as his whipping boy in hopes of becoming the next mayor of the city based on his stance. That was his goal, so there was nothing I did that was right. It didn't matter what the data showed, the board was data-proof.

"As much as I loved that institution and what its original mission was, that mission couldn't be met anymore. I decided, 'This is not a place I can work because I cannot do my job,' and I resigned." In retrospect, Moses realizes that she did not have a true grasp of the institutional context and underestimated the challenges of leading "a public institution in a highly politicized environment.

"CCNY in New York City is an institution of that city. It's a part of the city's history and legacy. I was drawn to those characteristics—not the office of the presidency. It was a unique experience.

"The presidency has its limits, and it isn't necessarily the place where you're going to make the kind of changes that you want. It's where the buck stops and you catch all the hell. You're constantly on, you're in the limelight all the time, and you have to figure out how to live that life and how to incorporate some sanity in it for yourself and your family."

Moses and her husband, James F. Bawek, have been married for more than 35 years and have two daughters. His career in the real estate industry allowed him to continue his work wherever his wife's job took them, and he was able to be at home for the girls when she couldn't be. "Our children understood and grew up with me doing these jobs, and I had a husband who was very much a partner in all this." Today, their eldest daughter, Shana, is an employment law attorney and mother to their first grandson. Youngest daughter Antonia is a recruiter and trainer for a large national organization.

"When we were at CCNY, the Harlem community wanted a liaison with the institution. I gave them my husband. At first, they thought I was joking because my husband is White. But we worked with the community to take back St. Nicholas Park, a big park that was set between the campus and the subway. This park had been taken over by drug dealers. My husband was our point person and during the years we were at CCNY, he won the community over. By the end of my term as president, community groups called him before they called me. When we left, they had a big party for him and put his name on a plaque on the fence at the park gate."

Moses has used her leadership and organizational skills in a variety of settings throughout her career. A member of the Board of the American Anthropological Association (AAA), she became its first African American president in 1995 and helped author the 1998 AAA's Statement on Race. She has been active in the American Council on Education (ACE) Office of Women for the majority of her career, and in 2007 she received the prized American Council on Education's Donna Shavlik Award for her lifetime commitment to advancing women and women's leadership in higher education. She also serves on the Board of Trustees of the Ford Foundation, the organization that in some respects set her direction by awarding her a doctoral fellowship.

"I think we still live in a society where leadership is seen as a male domain, so women are pushing against a norm. It may be more nuanced, it may be not as blatant as it was a decade ago, but there's still an assumption that leaders are males, and that if you're a woman, you must be exceptional in some way. You can't be just ordinary. Male leaders can be ordinary. Then there's the double whammy of being both female and African American and overcoming the assumption that you got there by means other than your own merit, that you are an affirmative action hire, or that 'they' had to have some diversity. I've been dealing with that my entire career, in every position that I've taken. The assumption is that somehow I was put there because I was a woman and/or I was a minority and they needed to have a woman or a minority in the position."

Following her tenure at CCNY, Moses completed a three-year term as president of the American Association for Higher Education (AAHE) in Washington, D.C. Although she was nominated for the University of New Mexico presidency and became a finalist (the position was filled by an internal candidate), Moses for the most part has chosen not to apply or be nominated for presidencies. "I looked around at a lot of other presidencies and decided that's not what I wanted to do. What I really want to do is to have a place where we can try to answer some of the unanswered questions around issues of leadership and diversity and higher education." She found that opportunity at her alma mater, the University of California, Riverside, to which she returned in 2003 as professor of anthropology, associate vice chancellor for excellence and diversity, and vice provost for conflict resolution. In these roles Moses has been assisting Riverside in developing a diversity strategic framework that will "increase the synergies" between the university's diversity initiatives and its other missions. The goal is "to build excellence in curriculum, programs, research and service by building on diversity of ideas, backgrounds, and cultures."

Moses's efforts to address these issues aren't confined to her campus. Recently, she helped launch The RACE Project, a new public program that expands on the AAA's 1998 Statement on Race. According to AAA's website (www.understandingrace.org), the program exposes students to "differences among people and reveals the realities—and unrealities—about race" through interactive and engaging activities. Her next goal is to develop a center for the study of diversity in higher education and society. "What I'm doing at Riverside, I had the potential to do ten years ago at City College. There was just not the opportunity or the environment to do it. Change comes very hard, and these kinds of changes take time; you just don't do them overnight"—a fact to which Yolanda Moses can readily attest because she has spent a lifetime making change, making things happen.

BIBLIOGRAPHICAL NOTE

The author conducted in-depth interviews with Dr. Moses and relied on the following sources for additional information:

A framework for diversity at UCR, The University of California Riverside (2004, May). Retrieved March 16, 2008, from http://www.diversity.ucr.edu/programs/community/initiatives.php

Arenson, K. (1999, July 2). City College president forced out by CUNY trustees under Badillo. *New York Times*, p. A1.

Glazer, N. (1999, July 11). What the CUNY-bashers overlook. *New York Times*, p. WK17.

McFadden, R. D. (1993, May 25). More a builder of bridges than a typical scholar. *New York Times*, p. B2.

Mydans, S. (1993, May 31). Taking the challenge as City College chief. *New York Times*, p. 25.

Newman, M. (1993, May 25). A new president for City College. *New York Times*, p. A1.

CHAPTER DEDICATION

To my husband Jim, who gave me an extraordinary life for 28 years before losing his life to brain cancer. His unfaltering love for me and our five daughters and his relentless support for my work and success provided an amazing foundation of strength and encouragement. He will forever be our hero.

AUTHOR BIOGRAPHY

Angela Hernquist, Ph.D., comes from an academic (B.S. and M.B.A.) and professional background in business and currently teaches in both the Higher Education Leadership and Women's Studies programs at the University of Nevada, Las Vegas.

SIX

CHOOSING A COMMITMENT TO CHANGE

Beverly Daniel Tatum
Spelman College

"IN 1991, I HAD A SPIRITUAL AWAKENING that has informed my choices ever since and has given further balance to my life. I sensed myself being called to antiracist education in which I was engaged at the time and still am today. I had and still have a desire to help change attitudes and behaviors through mutual understanding and a growing appreciation of what we all contribute to society. I began to think about the gifts that I had been given and to ask how I could best steward them and use them for the greater good. There have been times in my life since then when I have asked: Is this really the best use of my particular talents? Is this really what God is calling me to do? When I got the sense that what I was doing was fine, but not the most effective use of these gifts, I moved on to something different. I have tried to inform all of my major life decisions with this process of discernment. I think it has increased my effectiveness and allowed me to positively impact more people. It led me to choose to be a college president and, in particular, to be president at Spelman.

~ 77 ~

"I had the good fortune of having Barbara Brown Zikmund [nicknamed BBZ] as my advisor at Hartford Seminary, where I pursued a master's degree in religious studies. In 2000, as I was finishing up my program, she asked me about my career plans. At the time I was serving as the chief student affairs officer at Mount Holyoke and had been nominated for several presidencies but hadn't pursued any of them. BBZ was retiring after a ten-year presidency at Hartford Seminary and gave me this advice: 'A lot of people think you can be a president of just any institution, but it doesn't really work that way. First of all, institutions find you, you don't find them. Second, you can only be a president of an institution that you truly love because it's such a demanding role. It's a 24/7 job. But,' she said, 'you will do a lot for your lover.' I thought, 'What a great analogy.' You are in many ways married to the institution. When I was inaugurated at Spelman, it was like a wedding, all the pomp and circumstance and vows. Cornel West says that you can't lead the people unless you love the people, and I think you can't lead the institution unless you love the institution. You have to be passionate. A sense of calling helps generate the stamina, energy, and resilience you need to do the job. To be effective, you have to be totally committed. Now I don't walk around thinking, 'Oh, I'm so passionate.' But get me started, and I can go on a long time about what it is we're trying to accomplish at Spelman and why it's important," she laughs.[1]

"The mission of the institution is so powerful—preparing Black women for leadership, women committed to promoting positive social change—that I am continually inspired to do whatever I can to ensure that we provide nothing less than the best learning environment for them. Spelman is such a unique institution with such a distinguished history—it truly is a national treasure, and I feel the weight of the responsibility to preserve and strengthen this college for generations to come. Serving as president is not just a job, it truly is a calling, and responding to that call has been deeply satisfying."

Commitment to an educational calling might be in Beverly Tatum's genetic makeup. "I am a fourth-generation college educator. My grandmother's father, William Hazel, was a professor of architecture at Howard University. He was, in fact, the first dean of the School of Architecture at Howard. Both his mother and father taught at, and headed, the Cardinal Gibbon Institute, a Catholic institution that no longer exists but was modeled after Tuskegee Institute and located outside of Baltimore, Maryland. My father is a retired professor who specialized in art education.

"I was born in Tallahassee, Florida, in 1954 while he worked at Florida A&M. I call myself an 'integration baby' because I was born four months after the Supreme Court outlawed 'separate but equal' education based on race in *Brown v. Board of Education.* We moved to Massachusetts in 1958, when my father took a job at Bridgewater State College, becoming its first African American professor. My mother was a homemaker when I was small. But after we moved to Bridgewater, she pursued two master's degrees, one in elementary education and the other specializing in reading. After she graduated, when I was about eleven, she worked as a teacher in the local public schools.

"I am the second of four children. We grew up in Bridgewater, which is a small town about thirty miles from Boston. We were one of the few Black families in the town. For most of my growing-up experience, I was the only Black kid in the class, one of the few Black children in the school. I started school early, skipping kindergarten, and starting first grade just before my sixth birthday. Then I skipped the second grade, and graduated from high school when I was sixteen. I've had a high level of academic success throughout my life. And that, of course, opens doors for you.

"My oldest brother is a jazz musician. He attended Berklee College of Music in Boston and moved to Italy after he finished school. He still lives there with his Italian-born wife and son. My sister attended College of the Holy Cross in Worcester, Massachusetts. Today, she and her Irish-Catholic husband and their children live in the Boston area, where she is a professional fundraiser. My younger brother went to Rensselaer Polytechnic Institute and then the Art Institute of Chicago, where he earned an M.F.A. He has worked as an art professor but currently alternates between working as an artist and as a software engineer.

"I'm married and have two sons. My husband, Travis, is a retired college professor who spent much of his academic career at Westfield State College. Our oldest son, Travis Jonathan, is enrolled in a Ph.D. program in social psychology at my alma mater, the University of Michigan. If he decides to become a professor, he'll be the fifth generation. David, our youngest son, is at the University of Maryland, Baltimore County, in the Meyerhoff Scholars Program, studying the philosophy of science."

Effective leaders such as Beverly Tatum possess the stamina, energy, and resilience needed to answer their calling to the presidency. "I am an energetic person. You need energy to do this job. I maintain my energy in a variety of ways. I pay attention to what I eat. This job is hazardous to one's health from a nutritional standpoint because you attend a lot of social events involving food. People are feeding you all the time. If you're not paying attention, you can gain two, three, or four pounds a year, which doesn't sound like much. But if you gain two, three, or four pounds a year for ten years, that's forty pounds! I am fortunate to be a healthy person, but I need a certain amount of sleep. I'm a night owl. I usually go to bed around midnight. Some presidents tell you, 'I'm up at four in the morning.' I think to myself, you must go to bed at nine. I'm usually not out of bed before seven o'clock. When I get up, I exercise. I like to walk outside on campus, but I also use a treadmill. I have a spiritual life. There was a time when I would meditate, write in my journal, or just sit still, maybe for as long as an hour. I now find that it's hard to take that much time and also exercise, so I try to combine them. When I'm walking, I'm thinking to myself and having a little conversation with God, appreciating the beauty and the blessings in my life.

"It's important to have the right kind of support because it, too, impacts your energy levels. We moved to Atlanta from Massachusetts. Originally, I thought we would sell our house right away, but we decided to keep it for the first few years. It was a blessing to be able to escape for a long weekend. No one there cared that I'm the president of Spelman [laughing]. I could go to the grocery store in my jeans and not worry that I'm not looking presidential, and it was unlikely that I would run into somebody who would ask about his or her daughter's application to our college. My particular role at Spelman is highly visible and it is nice to be anonymous sometimes. It's hard to be anonymous in Atlanta. I rarely go anywhere in Atlanta where there isn't somebody who recognizes me and wants to talk to me. We did eventually sell our house in Massachusetts and decided to buy a condo in Atlanta because we really like the city, and over time, we were traveling back to Massachusetts less and less. The condo offers a different kind of escape, but it still serves that purpose. Now my Massachusetts friends come here to visit me.

"A friend of mine once told me, 'The work that you do requires withdrawals, psychological and emotional withdrawals of energy.

If you make a lot of withdrawals, you have to make a lot of deposits.' I can always tell when my deposit and withdrawal balance is out of whack. My introversion reveals itself in what I call over-stimulation. Being with a lot of people day after day starts to drain the energy out of me. When I have had too much contact, I need to get away and be by myself. The time alone helps me restore my balance. It can be sitting in my home office going through paperwork or listening to music. I enjoy time alone. It's one of the things I like about traveling. I'm in hotel rooms by myself. Even on planes, I experience myself as alone because no one interrupts me. Alone time is very important to me. I'm lucky that I have a wonderful husband who really understands that about me. He likes to be in my company, but he doesn't have to be in the same room. He likes knowing that I'm in the house, but if I want to sit by myself in another room, it's fine with him. He doesn't feel neglected.

"I couldn't do what I do every day without his love and support. He truly is my biggest fan and my closest confidant. It is true when they say, 'It is lonely at the top,' but my husband is a wonderful companion, always willing to listen and offer wise counsel when I need him to do that. He has always been actively involved in the care of our sons and he shares in the life of the Spelman community, hosting special guests and attending campus events with me or, sometimes, on my behalf. This experience too has just become another part of our partnership. Because my husband has been such a great partner and a devoted father, I have been able to balance being a mother and having a very demanding career."

But passion, energy, and loving support alone are not enough. "Clearly, as a leader, I must be competent, particularly as a Black woman. I can be as passionate as I want to, but if I'm incompetent, I'm not going anywhere [laughing]. I can't be effective, at least not in the long run. I suppose I could use smoke and mirrors for a while, but when things got complicated or when I really needed to understand what I was doing, if I were not competent, I'd start to make mistakes that were large enough for others to notice.

"Experience helps. When I graduated from college (I finished in December, a semester early), I took a job as a management trainee for Sears, Roebuck. It seemed like a good thing to do while I was waiting to see if I was going to get into graduate school. For about three months, they sent us to all the different parts of the organization, a week in customer service, a week in telephone sales, a week in the children's department, and so on, the point being that, when we finished, we understood the big picture in terms of the organization and how it operated. The last three or four years that I spent at Mount Holyoke College provided a similar experience. I was a member of a senior administrative team reporting to the president. We met for three hours every week. We worked well together. I learned not only about my job but everybody else's job because I was at the table when the VP for institutional advancement spoke about fundraising challenges, when the provost brought up faculty dilemmas, and when the CFO talked about budget issues. That breadth of exposure and knowledge has served me well as Spelman's president.

"The more opportunities you have to work in different parts of the institution, the better. My route to the presidency has been extremely valuable to me. I started out as a faculty member, and moving up through the ranks gave me knowledge about the tenure and promotion process. I know what it's like to chair a department and understand what a challenge it can be to hire new faculty because I've done it. I've worked with students as a therapist at a campus counseling center, so I learned about issues that students bring to campus. I was a chief student affairs officer for a number of years. I learned a great deal about students when I worked with them in the classroom, but I learned new things about them when I worked in student services. And finally, just prior to coming to Spelman, I served as acting president of Mount Holyoke for six months.

"Although competence gained through experience is important, there are smart people who are not effective leaders, at least in part because they don't understand people. I'm a psychologist by training, and I think it helps. I'm a pretty good communicator. I can connect personally, read people, and respond appropriately. It's a valuable skill. It's hard to imagine being an effective leader if you can't communicate. People look to the leader for the key messages about the organization and where it's headed. Being able to communicate in a way that engages them and excites them is terrifically important.

"One of my concerns when I first came to Spelman was that there was not enough college-wide communication. Sometimes it seemed that the left hand did not know what the right hand was doing. We created an e-mail newsletter as a way of providing an exchange of information. It goes to the whole campus— faculty, staff, and students—as well as to our alumnae. We use e-mail extensively; it's a powerful instrument. We also have some administrative structures, like a middle-management leadership council and a staff council, for example, that give me the opportunity to share information.

"I prefer written communication." Tatum's skill in writing has been widely acknowledged. She is described as one of 'our most persuasive and engaging commentators on race.' In each of her books and numerous articles and essays, she combines policy analysis with personal reflection and storytelling to raise questions about isolation in *Assimilation Blues*, identity in *Why Are All the Black Kids Sitting Together in the Cafeteria?*, and inclusiveness in her 2007 *Can We Talk About Race?* In this latest book, she warns of an ever-encroaching resegregation of America and raises questions about the nation's readiness to talk honestly about the continuing, contentious nature of race. Although she views her presidency at Spelman as God's calling, striving to affect U.S. race relations continues to fuel her professional and academic passion. As a reporter for the *Boston Globe* put it, "What Tatum seeks to do above all else is trigger discussions about race and inform those discussions with a reality-based focus on how race affects us all. Her latest book does that beautifully, asking touchy questions and patiently, inclusively seeking answers."

Tatum does suggest that her choice of medium depends on what she's trying to communicate. "Speaking in public is definitely not a natural skill for me. I am an introvert by nature. I was a shy child. All through school, I was the last one to raise my hand in class. I have outgrown my shyness, for the most part, but I still have to work at feeling comfortable in a room full of strangers. So public speaking is not something that I ever imagined I would be good at. I'm at ease with it today because I've practiced. As a professor, I learned to speak in front of people. And I spent many years conducting 'unlearning racism' workshops, as a social justice educator or what I call an 'antiracist educator.'

"Talking to people about race generates anxiety. It generates mine, it generates theirs because it almost always implies a need to change. I found that it helped if I spoke directly, not from notes, and if I stood away from the podium. When you stand behind a podium, there's a kind of distance between you and the audience. When I stood as close to people as possible, it had a certain disarming effect. In those situations, people were less likely to attack me; maybe I looked more vulnerable, and therefore they were less willing to take potshots. I do know that it helps people feel more connected. As president, I use that strategy as frequently as possible. For example, when I speak to alumnae, I rarely use notes. If I'm really trying to convey important ideas in a formal setting, however, I may want to be very precise with my language. I want to choose my words carefully; I write out what I'm going to say; and I usually do not veer from the text. But, when I can, I do like to speak without notes because it conveys a certain kind of sincerity. People can see, 'She's speaking from the heart.'"

Although Tatum believes that her honest, straightforward manner resonates best in what she typically refers to as dialogues or conversations about race, her ability to convey similar sentiments rings true in her writing as well. She continually makes her voice heard as she raises questions. In a *Washington Post* essay, she spoke pointedly about the continued battles in this country over "contested space in a toxic racial climate." She compared events in Jena, Louisiana, in 2007 to those in Little Rock, Arkansas, 50 years earlier and lamented the lost possibilities for creating a more civil, caring environment in this country and the violence that ensued in Jena because no one engaged in dialogue around our racial history.

Any dialogue requires listening. "You have to be a good listener; you have to listen to what's on the minds of other people before you tell everybody what's on your mind. As Stephen Covey says, you should first seek to understand and then to be understood. People want to be understood for who they are and what's important to them, and whether you're talking about fundraising or just talking about managing the people in your office, respecting and honoring people's individuality is important. You have to recognize their particular talents as well as their needs.

"Of course, there are times when I am the one who speaks first, perhaps laying out an agenda; but even then, I think about how I answer community concerns. When I arrived at Spelman in 2002, I spent a great deal of time talking to people about what they did and what they thought was important for me to know about their jobs, and I asked them what five things I should know about future development. That input helped shape our strategic issues. In general, the idea of making sure that you've heard what other people are saying before you try to tell them what you think is a good strategy.

"I try to be tactful. If I am upset, I let the person that I am upset with know, but I rarely embarrass people, especially in public. I attribute my tactfulness to my mother, who, when I was growing up always said, 'If you don't have something nice to say, don't say anything at all.' I've modified that advice: If you don't have something nice to say, say it nicely. It's not that I'm not going to address whatever the issue is, but I prefer to speak about it later one-on-one. In my first year at Spelman, an e-mail lambasting an employee circulated anonymously. In effect, it amounted to character assassination. When I learned about it, I was very upset, and I wrote an e-mail to the whole campus community, entitled 'Civility at Spelman.' In it I wrote, 'I cannot confirm that the e-mail accurately conveys what So-and-So did or didn't do. I can confirm that this e-mail is inappropriate. The person who sent it shouldn't have sent it; the rest of us had the option to delete it instead of passing it on. I expect that people will be treated with respect. If that's not the case, then somebody needs to come and talk to me about it.' Then I had a chat with the person about whom the e-mail was circulated. I said, 'I don't know whether these things are true; we're just getting to know each other, but I certainly want to communicate to you that I hope not because I cannot condone it.' This individual had a lot to offer, but also had a quick temper and sometimes used foul language when angry. I simply communicated that such behavior was not civil and that we have standards of civility. That individual changed that behavior.

"One of the challenges a leader confronts is to allow other people to do their work. You have to recognize when you are in the way. You don't want to micromanage people. On the one hand, you have to be focused. There are the day-to-day things that have to happen. If I spent all my time in the future, the present wouldn't get done. On the other hand, the future is the result of today's decisions, and so I have to have a plan in terms of where we're headed, and I have to know how that plan will be operationalized. In other words, if this plan requires me to do these things tomorrow, then what do I have to do today to be ready for that tomorrow? You have to continually weigh one against the other. If I am focused on the minutiae, then I can't think clearly about the bigger picture. I can't be at *every* function bringing greetings and still get my work done [laughing]. My primary responsibility is to identify the needs, prioritize those needs, set the agenda for the institution, and then move that agenda forward.

"For instance, in our current fundraising effort, we are focused on increasing financial support for our students, endowment support for faculty positions, and on the maintenance and preservation of the campus itself. But we also need to build a new arts building. This building is tremendously expensive and not affordable at this time, but I know we need it, even if we can't build it for another ten years. So I focused on our immediate goals—scholarships, faculty positions, and campus maintenance—but I also laid the groundwork for this future need. I let people know about it. I help people get excited, so they will ask: 'How can I help?' And I reply, 'As a matter of fact, down the road, we're going to need a hundred million dollars for a new arts building.'

"As a leader, it's also important to be viewed as accessible and at the same time to keep your ear to the ground. It's a way to know what's going on. I am at a small organization, approximately twenty-two hundred students and about seven hundred employees. I like to walk around campus. If it is early in the morning, I have a chance to meet and greet maintenance workers at shift change and public safety folks as they open up the campus. I speak to people. I want people to feel that, if they have a problem, they can stop me on the sidewalk and say, 'Dr. Tatum, I wanted to talk to you about X.' The students certainly do. If people are not stopping me, I need to have colleagues who will say, 'I was in the cafeteria and people were buzzing about X,' so I can head off trouble—nip things in the bud before they get to the point where it feels like a crisis.

"I travel quite frequently, but when I am on campus I try to maximize my visibility. For instance, I might go to a basketball game, or, even though I fly back to Atlanta on Friday and leave again on Sunday, I will attend a dance recital on Saturday night. I pass through the cafeteria and have lunch there once a week. I just show up at events, even if I can't stay long. Showing up is worth a lot of points, and I try to collect my points whenever I can [laughing].

"It builds credibility. People have to trust their leaders. You have to have integrity. I suppose, in the short term, someone could get things done by manipulating people or by lying, cheating, or stealing. But, that would catch up with you. Honesty counts for a lot. You also must be intellectually credible. If you are the leader of a college or university, it helps tremendously to have some academic credibility of your own. It helps you gain the respect of faculty.

"I came here with a great deal of credibility. I had a national reputation in terms of my scholarly work, in particular my book,

Why Are All the Black Kids Sitting Together? I'd also been at Mount Holyoke for thirteen years and had a solid track record there. But all of my work had been at predominantly White institutions. Some people here questioned my credibility as it related to a historically Black college. I'd never attended one, I'd never worked at one, and there was a sense among some people of, 'Well, she's been good in those *other* places, but we're different' [laughing]. When I first started, I often referenced my previous experience when people asked me questions. I'd say, 'Well, at Mount Holyoke we did such-and-such.' I got feedback that I was mentioning that 'other' institution a little bit too much. So I used to joke about it. I would say, 'Well, at the institution that shall not be mentioned . . .' [laughing]. But I did try hard not to begin every sentence with, 'Well, at Mount Holyoke,' because this is not Mount Holyoke, it's Spelman."

Spelman and Mount Holyoke hold similar places in the history of women's education. While Mount Holyoke is the oldest continuing U.S. institution of higher education for women, Spelman is America's oldest historically Black college for women. Both began as female seminaries. Spelman started as the Atlanta Female Baptist Seminary in 1881 and later changed its name to honor Laura Spelman Rockefeller, wife of John D. Rockefeller, who helped fund the school. Today, Spelman's students hail from 41 states and 15 foreign countries, and the college enjoys a national reputation for quality education. Tatum is the ninth president of this private, independent college, which currently is the only historically Black college to rank among *U.S. News & World Report*'s top 100 U.S. liberal arts colleges.

"I continually work at gaining credibility by demonstrating my appreciation for the Spelman traditions in tangible ways. For example, today I'm wearing light blue. It's the school color. Whenever I represent the institution, I wear blue—different outfits, but the same color combination. On the cover of my most recent book, I am wearing blue. I have a lot of blue clothing [laughing]. And, at Spelman events, it is common to sing the Spelman hymn. So, at my very first convocation, I felt it was important to come dressed in blue and to be prepared to sing the Spelman hymn without looking at the words. I worked hard to memorize the song, and when it came to the end of the convocation, my first public appearance at Spelman, we sang the song. Later numerous alumnae said, 'I was so impressed that you knew the song.' It helped me earn credibility.

"Commitment, competence, and credibility are the mainstays of leadership, but there are fundamental ways of thinking—intellectual, emotional, and interpersonal—that facilitate getting the job done. For instance, you have to kill your ego. There are a lot of temptations when you're in a powerful role. You must resist them, particularly greed and glory. We are all vulnerable to worshiping these gods. The god of greed is about our hunger for material things. I accumulate as much stuff as the next person, but I have never been status-driven. I'm not label-conscious. I actually try to simplify my life when it comes to possessions. I've learned to ask myself three questions about the things I acquire or choose to keep: is it truly useful, is it something I will truly enjoy, and does it give me positive energy? By positive energy, I mean does it relate to important parts of my life—as a parent, teacher, president of Spelman, traveler, African American, person of faith, or member of the Daniel-Tatum family. If the answer to these questions is no, I get rid of it.

"The god of glory is a little different story [laughing]. It's not that I aspire to be a famous person, but there's a way in which people flatter you. They say, 'You have to be here, you must do this, we can't function without you.' If you believe it, you're in trouble. You get stretched more ways than you can handle. This can happen at a place like Spelman because historically Black colleges seem to be more president-centered than predominantly White ones are. Initially, I wanted to be everywhere, so I could learn the organization and get to know people. But if I have to be in all those places, touching all those things, I can't do what I'm really supposed to do, which is lead the institution. Not succumbing to the belief that you are indispensable takes self-discipline.

"You also must be self-confident. Who could do this job without some sense of confidence? But at the same time, you don't want to be arrogant. You can't believe your own press releases. I have very little tolerance for people who are arrogant, and I certainly don't want to be viewed as conceited. Self-monitoring, self-controlling, and maintaining your core principles serve as preventatives against self-aggrandizement.

"Certain aspects of Spelman's culture promote a susceptibility to pride. When I first came to Spelman, I was struck by how deferential everyone was to me. I thought of the people I worked with as colleagues, and it became clear that they thought of me as 'the boss.' I really don't like that word—it conjures images of the overseer of a plantation for me, and that's not my style at all. I recognize that I am the leader, but I prefer to use the power of persuasion rather than the power of position to get things done. I have an informal style, and I call everyone by their first names, with a few exceptions. I think of us as all in this work together, and I encourage my co-workers to call me Beverly. It took quite a while before that began to happen, and I know there are many people who will never call me anything other than 'Dr. Tatum.' I recognize that the very idea makes them uncomfortable, and I don't push it.

"Initially I found patterns of interaction to be very rigid and hierarchical. There are some things about my life here that still feel that way, but I have gotten used to it. For example, I have a driver. That's a very useful thing. I don't have to look for parking spaces, I can get dropped off, get picked up, that's great, particularly in Atlanta traffic. But, it's very clear that I'm supposed to sit in the back of the car, and he's supposed to sit in the front. It makes me feel a little like we're reenacting *Driving Miss Daisy*, only it's Driving Ms. Beverly. I also know that he would be very uncomfortable if I didn't sit in the back. And my driver always opens the door for me, which is the part that I really have trouble with. It's sort of a joke between us because he and I know that it's a challenge for me to wait. He wants to get out of the car, walk around, and open the door for me. By the time he has done that, I could've been out of the car and down the street [laughing]. But it's very important to him that he open that door and help me out of the car, so I have learned to count to ten [laughing]. It's a part of the institutional culture, and perhaps Southern culture, and I just have to go along with it. If I didn't, he would feel devalued. Sometimes, I'm really in a hurry, and I'll just open the door, and I'm almost out before he gets to it, and I'll say, 'Oh, I'm so sorry, I forgot [laughing].'

"Culture can be understood in several ways. There's institutional culture; there's the societal culture, which may or may not match the institutional culture; and there's your own culture, which might be mediated by your racial or ethnic background and your own socialization. My institution definitely has a culture. Every institution does. Spelman has a very deep religious culture, or maybe spiritual is a better word, but it expresses itself in terms of religiosity. For example, if you're at a public meeting and food is served, there's a clear community expectation that someone needs to bless the food. You can't just get the food and bless it yourself. It needs to be a public blessing. If nobody's there to do it, I do it because everybody waits until it is done. That's particular to the Spelman culture. It doesn't necessarily reflect wider societal expectations where people just go and eat. But, I grew up in a family where it was customary to sit down and wait for somebody to bless the food before we started eating. So, on the one hand, in this respect my personal experience matches up with the institution's culture. I'm comfortable with it.

"On the other hand, my own life experience has been shaped by a variety of influences, and one of those influences is my experience at Hartford Seminary. There, I learned the importance of creating an inclusive environment for people of all backgrounds, all faiths, all traditions. So, if we're going to bless the food, we need to do it in a way that includes the Christians in the room (of all denominations) as well as the Muslims, the Jewish people in the room, the Bahá'ís in the room. To end every prayer, 'in the name of Jesus' leaves a lot of people out. Many members of this community come from religious traditions where this language is the norm. One of my goals has been to model for our students a more inclusive way of doing it—how to honor one's own tradition and still include others.

"My actions have raised a few eyebrows. Take, for example, the first graduation that I officiated. It had been the practice to have a Scripture reading at the ceremonies. So we had a Scripture reading at the baccalaureate ceremony, but we also had a reading from the *Koran*. There were definitely some questioning looks, but no one came to me and said, 'You can't do it,' and I have continued to do it. I wanted the Muslim students and their families to feel a part of the ceremony just as the Christian students did.

"My own personal leadership style is quite collaborative. It's based on mutual respect and the gentle use of authority. I have created structures to support that kind of collaboration. We now have separate advisory councils for hourly staff, middle managers, and faculty. The hourly staff council was new, and the idea that they could have input was new. In addition, once or twice a year, I give a State of the College address in which I detail the budget and talk about the decisions we've made and why we've made them. I try to make the process as transparent as possible because sharing information empowers people. The culture here previously was one where the president knows and only the president knows. My position is, everybody should know.

"I understand that if I really want something to happen, as the president I can make it happen. My preference, however, is to reach a shared agreement. I resist giving orders even if a person wants me to. I'm a consensus-seeker. I want people to understand that I'm choosing not to give an order. The more autocratic, militaristic approach can be effective, but I think you garner greater loyalty, build more of a sense of ownership, and foster better morale when you engage in mutual consensus building. We've been able to get a great deal done using a more democratic process. And I do see others modeling their behavior after some of the things that I've done.

"I'm sure growing up female and African American influences how I do what I do. And I'm sure growing up as a Black female in a predominantly White community where I sometimes felt left out, particularly as a teenager, is part of why it is important to me to always include other people and to model inclusive behavior. That growing-up experience spawned my research interest in how African Americans who live in predominantly White communities live their lives and resulted in my dissertation, which was later published under the name, *Assimilation Blues*. When I left Bridgewater, I very much wanted the opportunity to be part of a Black community. I attended Wesleyan University at a time when it was actively recruiting Black students, and I participated in a precollege program for entering students of color the summer before my freshman year. It was a wonderful experience for me to be surrounded by other Black and Latino students and to immerse myself in that cultural experience. Not only was my friendship network in college almost exclusively Black, I also took a lot of African American studies courses, along with the courses I needed for my major in psychology. I worked closely with a Black female professor as an undergraduate teaching assistant in a course, called 'Black Behavior Patterns,' where I was introduced to racial identity theory, an area of interest that has been at the core of my scholarship ever since. In the context of all of these experiences, my own racial identity as a young Black woman really emerged. Because I grew up in a predominantly White community, by the time I got to college, I'd had a lot of experience interacting with White people. In college, I wanted to learn something else, and I did. I became what I would call 'bicultural,' and I think that has been a source of personal advantage for me throughout my adult life. I feel comfortable in both Black and White communities, and today I have a diverse group of friends. My work requires me to engage with people of all backgrounds, and I know how to do that. It is a definite advantage."

The Tatums sought to provide that advantage to their sons. When they moved to Massachusetts, they chose Northampton because it had a college town atmosphere but wasn't totally dominated by the local colleges, and was within reasonable commuting distance from their jobs. They lived in a neighborhood similar to the one in which Beverly grew up. They raised the boys in a predominantly White community but tried to compensate for any social isolation they experienced by placing them in situations that reflected positively on who they are as African Americans. When they realized that their sons would be the only Black kids in the local public school, they chose to enroll them in private schools that had a more diverse student population. They belonged to the Martin Luther King Community Church in

Springfield, where Beverly and her sons sang in the choir. They created a home environment rich in art, music, literature, and the celebration of African American life. As a consequence of their efforts as parents, as well as changes in legal and social norms, Beverly commented, "My sons assume access."

Beverly Tatum earned her access and to an extent believes that women seeking positions of authority still must do the same. She comments, "The college presidency is still a male-dominated activity, but increasingly you see female presidents stepping up to the plate and being given opportunities. Women do face unique challenges—family, childrearing, and marital status. Not all women have families, but certainly if you have a family, it can be formidable, the whole dual-career couple issue, for example. I'm fortunate in that my husband, who is older than I am, was able to retire from his job to join me in Atlanta. He seems happy in Atlanta, and so it's working well. But if he had been in a position that he didn't want to relinquish, and I had this opportunity, although I'm sure we would have worked it out, it certainly would have been more difficult. Juggling the dual-career situation is not peculiar to women. One might say that it's challenging for men as well. But the nature of our society is such that women as trailing spouses is a more common occurrence than men as trailing spouses. The second issue—childrearing—is definitely unique to women. I think it would have been impossible for me to function as a president if my children were young. It's certainly been made much easier by the fact that my kids are grown. A third, less recognized, challenge stems from marital status. If you are a single person, maintaining a social life in a highly visible role has to be hard. I imagine that would be true for men, too, but women seem to suffer more scrutiny."

In her 2007 convocation speech, Tatum commented, "So many issues disproportionately impact women and call for solutions generated by educated women." She had recently returned from a gathering of women's college presidents in Bellagio, Italy, which was sponsored by the Rockefeller Foundation. Twenty leaders from 12 countries discussed the importance and unfinished business of educating women for leadership. With these discussions and thoughts fresh on her mind, she called problem solving and analysis the "tools of liberation" and challenged her students, saying, "Attending Spelman is a choice to change the world." Beverly Tatum's life is about making choices. She never attended Spelman, but she has made the choice to make change in the world.

BIBLIOGRAPHICAL NOTE

Beverly Tatum's story is the result of intertwining the contents of lengthy interview transcripts with information gleaned from her inaugural speech, convocation addresses, and president's page and from Spelman's history (http://www.spelman.edu).

Other sources include:

http://www.facinghistory.org

Goldscheider, Eric. (2002, January 10). At home with Beverly Daniel Tatum. *Boston Globe*. Accessed from http:/www.eric goldscheider.com

Marklein, Mary Beth. (2004, May 16). Spelman president Beverly Daniel Tatum. *USA Today*. Accessed from http://www.usa today.com

Tatum, B. D. (1987). *Assimilation blues: Black families in a white community*. Westport, CT: Greenwood Press. (Reissued with new introduction by Basic Books, 2000).

Tatum, B. D. (1997). *Why are all the black kids sitting together in the cafeteria? And other conversations about race*. New York: Basic Books.

Tatum, B. D. (2007). *Can we talk about race?: And other conversations in an era of school resegregation.* Boston: Beacon Press.

Tatum, B. D. (2007, September 23). It's the same old story in Jena today. *Washington Post*, B03. Accessed from http://www.washingtonpost.com

seven

ENERGIZED FOR THE HARD WORK OF LEADERSHIP

Jerry Sue Thornton
Cuyahoga Community College

"ALMOST ANY CAREER PERSON must have passion for the work. I have a passion for education. Education has transformative power. It allows people to participate in a broader society, to be included, and to share. It is enabling and freeing. I chose to go into education because it's a ministry for me. Higher education—and especially community college education—is a calling. People hear my passion, they see it. It's in everything I do. My grandfather was Baptist minister in Tennessee. Fiery sermons were his mainstay. I learned a lot about the need for passion from the environment in which I grew up.

"I come from a coal-mining, farming family in western Kentucky. My mother had an eighth-grade education. My father went through the sixth grade. He worked the night shift in the mines and tended a small farm to support our family. I am the fourth of five Pritchett children. One of my sisters was able to attain a college education through the Army, and my brother did so through the Navy. I remember my father telling me that I was going to college. I said, 'I don't know how I'm going. We don't have the money.' He said to me, 'Well, you're so smart, you'll figure out a way to get there.'

"I was the first to go straight from high school to college. I received a small scholarship to Murray State University in Murray, Kentucky, which I supplemented with work. I got a job in the cafeteria, where I served breakfast from 6:30 a.m. to 8:30 a.m., went to class, came back and served lunch from 11:30 a.m. to 1:30 p.m., then went back to class in the afternoon, and returned to serve dinner from 4:30 p.m. to 6:30 p.m. Because I could sew and the Drama Department needed someone to make period costumes, I took on a second job in the evenings. The schedule was daunting, but I never considered quitting. If there are obstacles in the way, you don't concentrate on them. If you do, you'll never get to where you want to go.

"I have a very strong commitment to education because it was a big part of my moving from humble beginnings in rural Kentucky into middle-class status. Teachers played an integral role in my early life. They encouraged me to plan for a brighter future, one that I could only imagine. Education was the pathway to that future. It was the road to understanding life better, understanding and gaining information about and appreciation for things that I might not have had growing up."

After graduating college in 1969, Jerry Sue taught 6th-grade English in Earlington, Kentucky. This job was followed by a return to Murray, Kentucky, and a year of teaching 11th grade. During this time, she earned her second degree from Murray State University, a master's degree in communications. After that, she moved to Illinois and became an English instructor at Triton College. She taught there for six years before moving into the college's administration as an assistant dean, associate dean, and, finally, dean of arts and sciences. In 1983, during her stint at

Triton College, she earned a Ph.D. from the University of Texas at Austin and two years later moved to Lakewood Community College in Minnesota to become president of that institution.

"I left Chicago and moved to Minnesota, even though I didn't particularly want to leave Illinois. I knew no one in Minnesota, not a single person. But I was willing to pack my suitcase and start from scratch. I did so because at that time in Illinois the only female president of an institution of higher education (that wasn't Catholic) was Hanna Gray at the University of Chicago. And an increase in women in presidencies wasn't going to happen anytime soon in Illinois. I knew that if I wanted to be a president, I had to apply in states that were more open to having a woman, and an African American, frankly. Even today, you can find states where there are few, if any, female or African American community college presidents.

"I care deeply about community colleges. I don't see what I do as an everyday job but as a way of helping make a huge difference in the lives of others—enabling people to reach their goals, to have a better life. I started working at a community college in the fall of '71, and I have stayed in community colleges in three states, Illinois, Minnesota, and Ohio, for over thirty-seven academic years. I like being in the community college environment because it's where 'the rubber meets the road.' We are so close to our local communities. Our world is not just the institution; it includes the community. It's fun because it broadens the base. It gives a different flavor from what you find in the university world. I have had a couple of opportunities to move into the university setting or even into business, but this is the right niche for me.

"For community college presidents, not being involved in the community is not an option. It's the community's college. Whatever the issues, challenges, and struggles are for that community, they become a part of your institution. You are close to the community whether or not you want to be because the community feels ownership. We have a responsibility to respond to its issues. I've always enjoyed this part of the job, trying to assess the direction that the community might be going and how we can align the college with that direction. As president, I am very much a part of the community's leadership because forty-two percent of our funding comes from county support via the voters, another thirty-two percent from the state, and the rest from student tuition.

"When you choose to go into a leadership position in a community college, you have to understand the visibility requirements. You do everything on the public stage. The stamina, the energy that you have to have for these jobs is incredible. It is very similar to pastoring a church. It is twenty-four hours a day. And the extent to which you possess and demonstrate energy by participating and being involved and engaged determines whether or not people see you as the leader. I happen to be blessed with a lot of energy. As a kid I probably needed to be on medication. I have to monitor my energy level because sometimes what is a positive can also be a negative. It just depends on how you turn the prism. I have to be careful because I can wear people out. I can't always run in fifth gear.

"I don't require a lot of sleep. Yesterday, I was up at 5:30 a.m. and I was at work until 7:30 p.m. Then I went to a community event. I got home at 11:15 p.m. A lady at last night's banquet leaned over to me and said, 'I saw you last night.' I said, 'That's right.' Some weeks, I'm out every night; others it's three or four nights a week. My husband, Walter, often laughs and says, 'If I ever want to know where you are, all I have to do is call Wanda. Wanda knows.' Wanda is my administrative assistant. She keeps my calendar, both professional and personal.

"My personal and professional lives blend together in that my work activities provide some opportunities for personal enjoyment. Things that I like to do for fun often relate to my leadership role. I love sports, but I don't just go to a basketball or baseball game. I enjoy the symphony or a play, but my attendance is almost always in connection with some business for the college. Even while attending entertainment events, I am able to network for the college.

"The community college is an integral part of my family life. My husband and I view the college community as family. If you view yourself as split between work and personal life, then there is not sufficient time for either. Any balance between my career and personal lives derives from the fact that I love what I'm doing. I am energized by people and find that the college events and activities integrate nicely into my personal life. I knew the job's intensity when I went into it. It's not work. Even on vacation, I'm on the telephone, I'm thinking about work. It's fun; it's exciting. This is the job that I was born to do. I love it!"

In their 1998 book, *Prosperity: The Coming 20 Year Boom and What It Means to You,* Davis and Wessel included a discussion about how community colleges change lives. They used Cuyahoga as an exemplar and Jerry Sue's inaugural address theme, "The Community College as the Dream Catcher" as one of the chapter titles. "I first learned about dream catchers from Minnesota's Native American people. In a family with a newborn baby, a dream catcher [two or more circles of varying sizes joined together and crisscrossed by spiderweb-like filigree] catches the baby's good dreams and lets the bad dreams pass through it. Community colleges are the dream catchers for a vast number of people pursuing the American dream of financial stability and enjoyment of life—a better life.

"I care deeply about what faculty teach, how they teach, and, most importantly, about the success of our students. We have a contract with our students. We say, 'If you give us your hard-earned dollars, we will give you content and information. If you are willing to learn, we'll continue subject after subject until you get your degree.' Part of my job is to serve as a cheerleader. I was a cheerleader in high school, so I have experience. I cheer on our students. I cheer on the successes of people in their careers. I'm a cheerleader for people who are looking for second chances. That is the stuff of community colleges.

"Cuyahoga is Ohio's oldest and largest community college. It is a huge institution. When I was in St. Paul, there were seven thousand students on one campus. It was much easier. Here, I encountered the complexity of a multicampus community college with more than twenty-five thousand students and another twenty thousand people who come to us for workforce training. Cuyahoga's annual budget is almost twenty times larger than Lakewood's was at the time I was president. Its faculty and staff outnumber my faculty and staff in Minnesota ten to one. We have seven sites, four workforce training campuses, and three regular campuses. We spend a great deal of time branding the college as a single unit. To reinforce this one-college concept, we trademarked the college's acronym, Tri-C. Although we have different locations, students can expect some standardization, some consistency. As customers of the college, students can expect counseling, registration, enrollment mechanisms, and quality of instruction to be the same at all our sites. It's very much like you'd find at Nordstrom. I try to select team members who share this philosophy of quality and consistency because we'll never succeed in fulfilling our game plan for student success if we don't have people who have the same kind of commitment.

"I realize that everybody is not like me. As humans, we tend to think that everybody thinks the way we think, that everybody sees the world the way we see it, that we all have the same perspective, and that perspective is mine. And it just isn't true. People come from various regions and different economic backgrounds with different experiences that shape how they see the world, how they take in information. I can't create a oneness, a sameness of thought. I try to figure out a way to accommodate individual thinking and generate collective results. Not everybody's going to get everything they want, but how I negotiate through that, and how I get to solutions and places that people can accept, embrace, and move forward on, is important. As a leader, it's not always my ideas that win out. And they shouldn't. I love debating, and if you can make a good argument for why I'm wrong, I'll accept it and go in a whole different direction from where I started out. I laugh sometimes and think, 'How'd I get here?'

"I am introspective in my decision making and in my leadership. I take time to think through decisions. I constantly align the needs of our students with how we organize and how we fulfill the mission and purpose of the institution. I stay in touch with my own value system because we make decisions based on what we value. And we shift in our thinking with the years and with experience. What's important at one time becomes less so at another. For example, if you're a leader and you have a young family, you have a different set of values than when the kids are grown and gone. You have a different commitment. Knowing who you are, what you believe in, what you will and won't do, and how far you will and won't go is extremely important, because in leadership positions you certainly are going to be tried. I need to know my parameters before I get to those forks in the road. I want no surprises. If I understand the purpose for my behavior—

why I am doing this or why I'm aligned with that—it results in a far better decision and a greater chance for success.

"Over time, I've gotten to know the people I work with, to be able to predict how they think. I know who will think the exact opposite of how I'm probably going to think, and that's the first person I seek out because I want to hear what that person has to say. If you accept that you will never have everybody coming at an issue from the same point of view, it's much easier to figure out how to get to a collective vision. There's beauty in where you end up because you end up in a far better place.

"We subscribe to Dusty Staub's wholehearted leadership. I have trained most of the college, administrators, faculty, and staff, in its principles. It deals with the importance of intellect, but it also focuses on the necessity of emotional intelligence—understanding and having the capacity for empathy, having the ability to appreciate others' views, and incorporating those views in your decision making. Leaders fail because they don't possess or mature in their emotional intelligence. Parker Palmer in *Courage to Teach* says much the same thing. He asks: How can we best reach out to students as humans? How can we expect them to be successful learners if we don't appreciate and know them as learners? Faculty not only teach a discipline, they teach people.

"Working from this mindset helps you get people motivated. I watched Continental Airline go to the brink of bankruptcy. And I watched Gordon Bethune, its CEO—his philosophy and his style and his way of doing business. Continental came back because of the buy-in of everyone at Continental. Bethune made the mechanic, the gate attendant, and the stewardess believe that the company's success hinged on each of them as individuals. Xerox, too, almost went bankrupt. The company hired an external CEO thinking he could turn it around. He couldn't. Then Xerox brought in Anne Mulcahy, who'd been with the company for years and never envisioned herself as its CEO. A big part of her success was getting the people of Xerox to believe in themselves and in the company. And to deliver. To go back to why Xerox had been successful. To revive that spirit, work ethic, performance, and innovation. To bring Xerox back. It's that human factor. It's appreciation for what people know and what they can do, and how successful they can be for you.

"I suspect that minorities and women are sometimes good at this because we have had to study people; we've had to understand people better. There is no choice. If you don't have the power, and you're trying to reach your goal, you have to think about how the people whom you work and interface with think and act in order to get your job done. As minorities, we've had to watch and understand those in power a lot more than they've ever had to watch and understand us. It's a given. You do it to survive.

"Not only are very effective communicators observant, they are good listeners as well. It takes patience to let people get it all out and say what they think. Finding out what messages guide behavior in the organization, both formal and informal, is crucial. I learned that lesson in Minnesota. Minnesota is a very genteel state populated in large part by Scandinavian people who believe in saying things that are nice. Going from Chicago to Minnesota was a real culture shock. In Chicago people say what they think. You ask, 'How do you feel about such-and-such?' And they say, 'Well, I don't like it.' When I got to Minnesota, I discovered that that's not how people communicated. I might say, 'How do you like that idea?' And the reply might be, 'Oh, that's a great idea.' I could ask numerous individuals and get lots of compliments about that idea, but when I'd say, 'You think it might work?' The answer was, 'Well, no.' The Minnesota culture didn't embrace straightforwardness and directness. It wasn't something that was valued. Making the person feel good, feel positive, affirming the person, that's what was valued. The experience taught me that if I don't ask the right questions, I might go off thinking that I am on the right track when I'm not.

"Here at Cuyahoga, we spend a great deal of time discussing our options and analyzing our actions in formal meetings and retreats, but informal communication really gives me a better sense of what people think and whether or not they accept certain ideas or initiatives. It identifies 'itches' in the organization. I have lots of conversations with students and staff. I can be walking across campus and see one of the custodians. I'll stop and say, 'What's new, what are you doing, how's your family, what's going on,' and before you know it, they're telling me whatever it is that's on their minds. There's a comfort level in talking to me. I'm not the president of the college; I'm a fellow member of the community. There is a connection. People appreciate that I value their opinions and I'm interested. I keep my ear to the ground and stay open, listening. Sometimes I just swallow and accept what's being said. I have to remember to separate the message from the messenger, because if I kill the messenger, the messenger won't come back.

"You earn people's respect, you earn their trust. It's based on your behavior and the predictability of your behavior. People want to be able to predict, with some degree of certainty, what you will do, and in which situations you will protect them. They want to know that you're going to have their best interests at heart and that they can count on you to tell them the truth, even though it might be tough or not so pleasant. Now, behavior can be positive or negative. It goes both ways. They can look at you and say, 'This leader is going to lie to me on a regular basis because time after time she has.' People are very good observers of behavior, especially with leaders. Because they've given you the power and authority to lead them, to be their spokesperson, to be their advocate, they want some kind of comfort level. The more comfort that exists, the more power they will give you. For instance, when a board of trustees has little faith in a president or a chancellor, it tightens the rules and regulations. When it trusts you and what you do, it relaxes the policies that determine how you have to operate.

"As a leader you are an extension of those you represent. Everybody wants to have pride in whoever his or her leader is. 'Does this person represent me the way I want to be represented? Is there integrity in the decisions he or she makes?' If you do something out of character, there's a little jolt, and they look to see if it's an episode. 'Is there something going on in her life that I don't know about that's caused this action?' I serve on a corporate board[1] where not long ago the CEO did something that was unacceptable. He knew it right away. He's a golfer, and a number of the people on the board with me, men and women, are golfers. And because he was trying to save face, he said, 'I just did something that I'd like to ask for a mulligan on.' Everybody knew it was his way of saying, 'I made a mistake here; I let you down; I'm not going to do it again,' which he never would've said. Everybody makes mistakes. But if it starts looking like a particular action isn't a one-time thing, if it becomes the way in which you behave on a regular basis, that's when things start taking a different turn.

"Often, new presidents are anxious to prove themselves. They jump in and say, 'Gee, this needs to be done. This needs to be

---

1. Thornton serves on the boards of several national education organizations and is a board member and director of National City Corporation, American Greetings Corporation, RPM, Inc., American Family Insurance, and Applied Industrial Technologies, Inc. Locally, she is a board member of United Way of Cleveland, The Cleveland Foundation, Greater Cleveland Partnership, and the Rock and Roll Hall of Fame and Museum–Cleveland and New York.

fixed. We need to go in a completely different direction,' and they set off to do it. I've watched presidents of both colleges and universities do that and you just know they're going to crash and burn. It's so clear that they're moving at a pace that the rest of the institution can't handle, can't follow, and can't sustain.

"I watched a president come in and decide that he was going to make his institution a premier university, move it up right alongside Harvard. He decided to bring in top-notch professors who publish to build the institution's reputation and fired people to make room for the new ones. Well, everybody you fire has friends. It doesn't take long for it to start catching up to you and end your tenure. If you'd like to raise the academic status of the university, it has to happen over time with retirements, with openings created when people move on to something else. You're seeding the possibility and growing the reality all the time.

"You really need to assess the culture early on. You can't go in there with your solutions in your back pocket thinking, 'I've met this problem before when I was in Tennessee, and now I'm in New York, so I'm going to try the same thing.' It doesn't work, even within the same state, it doesn't work. Whatever the unit is, it can be a department or the full organization, you must learn its history. History is like a rubber band. The organization always pulls back to that shape. So find out what the challenges and issues over time have been, what people did to overcome them, what expectations the community and area hold, how people do business, how they dress, how they talk, what's expected, what's approved, what's not approved. When you do, you begin to put on the organization like a garment. It starts fitting you because you have what you need to determine how you're going to fit into and behave within the organization. Fit will determine whether you succeed or fail. It determines your longevity. It determines your happiness.

"You have to know what your organization will bear. It doesn't mean you aren't going to take risks, and it doesn't mean you aren't going to do the things that are absolutely right. You might have to step up and say this culture will never be open to this change, but it is the one we need. Kay McClenny always said that if you have to eat a frog, eat it early in the morning and get it over with. I'm beginning to think more and more that if you have to make decisions that are distasteful, bad, or painful for other people, the sooner you make them, the better. There've been a number of times when I've delayed letting someone go who I didn't think was right for the organization, hoping that he or she might become acclimated. In reality, that individual was not ever going to be the right fit for that particular job.

"Leaders in any industry, education, corporate America, the arts, or human services must be willing to take risks. It takes courage. You must put yourself out there, open yourself up for embarrassment or failure. You have to be assertive and have the confidence to move forward. It has to be a part of who you are, a part of your fabric. You gather as much information as you can and process it as collaboratively and inclusively as you can. But at the end of the day, the committee doesn't make the decision. You do.

"When I arrived in Cleveland, I found that the faculty were highly unionized. The community is highly unionized, so the community college has certainly taken on some of the culture of the community. I had to think through with others, who were longtime natives of the area, which aspects of that culture would help us and what would hinder or block us from meeting our mission of educating students. We asked what changes needed to be made, and how quickly or slowly they needed to be made because time is a real factor in a culture. Critics said I wouldn't last long. I knew when I arrived that it would take time to see change through to fruition. I would have thought it inappropriate to be here only three or four years. At that point you're just getting to know the landscape. Some things took many more years than we ever thought they would.

"For example, about five years prior to my arrival, all of the universities around us began moving from quarters to semesters, except for Ohio State University. We decided that we needed to investigate the possibility of making the same change. Our faculty dragged their feet. The liberal arts-humanities-type faculty wanted semesters; the career faculty wanted quarters. We had a stalemate. I finally said, 'We've studied this for two years, and now we've got to make a choice. My criterion for this decision is not going to be what the faculty want, but what's best for our students. And the decision is to move to semesters. The union responded, 'If you move forward, AAUP [American Association of University Professors] will issue a vote of no-confidence.' I replied, 'Do whatever you have to do, but I have to do what's best for the students and their ability to transfer to the university. That's the recommendation I intend to make to the board.' We have an appointed board. Its members tend to be people who care about the community. They are not wealthy. They are not trying to make a statement. They know the value of the community college to the students who come here and its value to the community. They look for me to make decisions that positively impact students. They see these as the best decisions I can make.

"They expect me to have a foot in each of two worlds. One in the present, where you are totally focused on what you're doing today, and what has to be achieved today, and what success means today. And the other foot in the future, where I am always scanning the environment to determine how I can take the institution forward. The new technologies, the speed of change, the differences between the students who are coming to us now and the ones who will be coming to us in the future, new ways of looking at the world, globalization and its impact on the college and its culture, the changes that are inevitable, that are going to take place with or without me, all have to be considered. I think and act innovatively and entrepreneurially." Under Thornton's guidance, Tri-C brought to fruition such efforts as its Virtual Open House, which affords students the opportunity for online live chats with counseling and financial aid personnel, and its successful Corporate College and Workforce Solutions, which provide advanced credit and noncredit training for a variety of corporations to enhance economic development in northeast Ohio.

"What's becoming more and more critical to our region and our country is the collective strength of a well-educated community. We must educate young students for emerging careers, train and retrain workers for jobs available now, and help white-collar professionals and executives work smarter. At Tri-C, we are creating new career programs, such as alternative energy technology, that align with the needs of our local business and industry. At the same time we are expanding the capacity of other programs, such as registered nursing, physical therapy, and culinary arts, all areas identified as having continuing growth in employment for the next several years. We continually expand our instructional delivery modes through distance-learning, weekend-college, and blended-learning modalities.

"I always anticipate the future but at the same time take care of the business of the day. When I became president in 1992, we had a bond issue. It was January and we were on the ballot in May. It's a perfect example of tending to the immediate needs of the institution in order to secure its future. Fundraising is a huge part of this job. You can't escape it, and, typically, you are not prepared for it. I had to learn the community fast and I had to get out there quickly because people vote for familiar leaders, for people they have confidence in. If they're going to give you their tax dollars for your institution, they want to know who you are and that you are a person of integrity who will spend those dollars in the right way. I took any opportunity that was offered to me to speak to the community—the PTA, Chamber of Commerce, radio shows, TV morning programs. People were interested because I was the new president. I was interested because I needed the exposure. I learned that we have to share the college with the community. It was a real eye-opening experience for me. Looking back on it, it was good that we had that bond issue so early in my tenure. I didn't feel that way at the time. It wasn't until after the bond issue vote that I had a chance to get to know the college better, but it did help me get to know the community. In 2005, Cuyahoga County voters passed our renewal levy by the second-largest margin in the college's history. I was out there again campaigning hard in the community. I was so focused that, while campaigning at the polls, I tripped over a manhole cover but never dropped my campaign sign and never stopped saying 'Vote for Tri-C,'" she laughs.

"As leaders, we often believe that we have to be invincible; we have to show that front of strength. And in doing so, we don't allow ourselves to be human. But followers accept people being human. If you never let people see that you are human, when you make a mistake, they say, 'Wait a minute, I don't accept that person being human because he's never been human before.' If you allow people to see that you're human like them, they don't feel that they have to hold you to that impossibly high standard that you've set for yourself. Now, you can't overburden them, but it's okay, from time to time, to show that you have aches and pains and hurts and parts of life that aren't so great. They empathize with you. They give you a little more leeway. I'm blessed with pretty decent health, and people here at the college are not used to my being sick. But last winter was hard. I had sinus infections, and a couple of times I couldn't talk for a week or two. People asked, 'Well, how are you doing?' I said, 'You know, I'm just trying to survive this winter.' 'Oh, I understand that,' they laughed. Old age is really something. I don't bounce back as fast as I used to [laughing]. In fact, one of our staff members was teasing me today. He said, 'You're going to have to give up that *American Idol* job if you can't sing anymore.' I said, 'I know, I'm going over to *Dancing With the Stars*'" [laughing].

Jerry Sue Thornton has been honored by women's, business, education, African American, Hispanic, Jewish, and Muslim groups. She garnered the Council for Advancement and Support of Education's (CASE) 2003 Chief Executive Leadership Award and was the 2006 recipient of the second American Council on Education (ACE) Council of Fellows Mentor's Award. She was also a 2007 honoree of Dominion's Strong Men and Women Excellence in Leadership program. This program honors African American men and women who are positive role models.[2]

She believes that nurturing and supporting future leaders must include a strong focus on executive professional development. "I encourage senior administrative staff to visit other community colleges to observe best practices and develop relationships with peers; participate in national conferences and share information with colleagues upon their return; as well as pursue continuing education and professional or doctoral-level education. In addition we provide opportunities for individuals with identified potential for advancement to serve in interim assignments where they can acquire additional expertise and exposure to other areas of the College."

---

2. Dominion, headquartered in Richmond, Virginia, is one of nation's largest producers of energy.

"Preparing new leaders who can assume the role of college president also requires fostering a culture where people feel empowered to grow personally and professionally, and to develop their decision making and leadership skills. I find it personally rewarding when I see educators and administrators progress in their careers and I find it deeply gratifying when I am privileged to witness their contributions to the field of higher education."

As Cuyahoga's first female president, Jerry Sue Thornton has proven to be a powerful force—dynamic, engaging, dedicated, self-assured. "Success," she says, "is garnered one step at a time. There is no elevator to the top. Hard work, commitment, and preparation are major parts of those steps. I tell people all the time that, when you find the right niche and you're in the sweet spot, that's when you can leave a legacy. Love what you do. I get so much joy out of the time that I'm giving."

BIBLIOGRAPHICAL NOTE

Jerry Sue Thornton's story is based on material gathered from interview transcripts; vita; Rick Haase's *From Coal Mines and City Streets to College President and Prime Time,* and the president's column, both of which appeared in the Spring 2006 issue of the *Tri-C Times*; and the following websites: www.dom.com/about/ education/strong/2007/thornton and http://www.tri-c.cc.oh.us/ home/default.htm.

eight

FOR THE GREATER GOOD

Belle S. Wheelan
Southern Association of Colleges & Schools, Commission on Colleges

"**D**URING SEGREGATION, my grandmother and great-aunt were businesswomen. My great-aunt owned a drugstore. When Lena Horne, Nancy Wilson, or Duke Ellington came to town, they'd stay at their house because the hotels were segregated. This was before I was born, but taking care of others was a value instilled in my childhood. All my life I've been like that house by the side of the road. I'm the same way in my job.

"When I come into an organization, I try to meet individually with each employee. I get to know the people. I know when their kids are sick, when a wedding is being planned, when a mom has just fallen and broken her hip. All of those things impact the way you work and your ability to work and whether or not your mind is on your work. If people aren't doing their jobs, it's important to understand why. Is it a competence issue, or is it because they're shuffling all this other stuff around? It's much more of a female than a male leadership behavior.

"I'm probably more laid-back and down-home in my leadership style than many people. Very seldom do I introduce myself as Dr. Wheelan because I believe it puts up barriers. I try to get rid of as much of the superfluous as possible just to make the relationship better. I want to gain respect as a person, not just for my professional position. That means your getting to know me, the person. I need to feel close to the people, and I need them to feel close to me. It's difficult because, as you move up in leadership, the fewer friends you have inside the organization. Once I became a campus provost, people stopped having lunch with me. Nobody wanted to go to lunch with the boss. If they're seen with you, they are perceived as either in trouble or brownnosing.

"Many leadership skills are learned early on. The way you are as a child is probably close to the way you're going to be when you're an adult. I was raised by a group of very strong women. I'm an only child. My mom and dad separated when I was six and divorced when I was twelve. I was raised by my mom in San Antonio. My grandmother, great-aunt, and one of my mother's sisters lived right next door to me. My mother was a public school teacher. She said she didn't want anybody who was mad with her to take it out on me, so, since we are Catholic, I went to Catholic school. I started school when I was four. I spent the first semester in kindergarten and the second semester in first grade. Then they promoted me to second grade at the end of the year. I was sixteen when I graduated from high school, twenty when I graduated from Trinity University in 1972 with a double major in psychology and sociology."

After earning an M.A. in developmental educational psychology at Louisiana State University, Belle worked at San Antonio College for 13 years. During that time, she continued her graduate studies and in 1984 received her Ph.D. from the University of Texas Community College Leadership Program, well-known for preparing community college presidents. "I was thirty before I decided to become a college president. I went from faculty to president in seven years." Her first presidency, which she held for six and one half years, came in 1992 at Central Virginia Community College. She was the first African American woman to lead an institution of higher education in the Commonwealth of Virginia. In 1998 she became the president of Northern Virginia Community College (NOVA), Virginia's largest institution of higher education and, at that time, the nation's second-largest community college.

"NOVA had sixty thousand students, five campuses, two thousand full-time employees, and another two thousand part-time employees when I became president. It was a big operation! The staff had not met together in one place in something like twenty-five years. So when I got there, I called a meeting of the faculty and administrators, and classified staff had their own meeting. Many of these people had been talking on the phone to each other for years and had never met because they worked on different campuses. It is useful sometimes to make the effort to get even a large group together occasionally to create a sense of community. And it is good to have everybody in one place to hear the leadership's message all at the same time, even though you know people are going to interpret it differently. I also funded projects that included faculty from all the campuses. It was the first way that the sense of community and culture started to change. Just getting people to talk to each other sometimes makes a big difference.

"Culture within the organization is certainly a factor in what a leader can do. My predecessor at NOVA had been president for thirty years. Changing an institution after a president had been there for so long meant that I had to get people working together because I couldn't do it by myself. When I arrived at NOVA, five distinct campus cultures existed, with everybody doing things differently. We didn't have a logo or common stationery or anything.

My predecessor had taken a map of the service region and literally drawn lines for each campus, saying, 'You market here, you market here, you market there.' Twenty-five, thirty years ago that probably worked. It doesn't work now with people living one place and commuting to work in another. Why shouldn't the people in the northern part of the community know about the programs offered at the campus in the southern part? I'm thinking, 'This is crazy! We've got programs dying over here because people over there don't even know they're available.'

"I felt it was important to change the culture to create a sense of one institution. The goal was to make it easier for the students, so many of whom were taking classes on more than one NOVA campus. We needed to get our act together, to have the same hours, to standardize the information going out to students, that sort of thing. I had to understand the culture, to recognize what the staff was accustomed to. That made all the difference in the world in trying to figure out how we were going to get them to change. That was why I started with the faculty, because if you can get the faculty on board, then everybody else tends to follow along. Faculty is the major component of the college culture, and you have to find a way to work effectively with them. I often took faculty with me when making a fundraising pitch or to the Chamber of Commerce meetings and meetings with the local school superintendents. They made presentations on their programs or projects about which we wanted to spread the word.

"It is important that everyone throughout the organization stays engaged and knows their value to the organization. Good leaders look for opportunities for staff growth and renewal. Staff who've been with the organization a long time sometimes figure, 'I guess this is all I can do.' One of the things I tried to do on search committees was to make sure that if the search was for a division chair, the secretary to that division chair was on the search committee. He or she works most closely with the new chair and, more than anybody, knows what the job really entails. I wanted that person involved. Exposing staff members to those kinds of opportunities and activities is always appreciated because they feel, 'Wow, I get to have some input.' Often, just exposing people to different activities will bring out their leadership qualities and rekindle their passion for the organization.

"Passion is contagious, I think. I'm passionate about everything I do. I believe if you're going to do something, you've got to feel it or you shouldn't be doing it. I'm not going to do something if I don't believe in it. As a leader, having passion for an organization means that everywhere you go, it's the first topic of conversation; all your thoughts, at least regarding work, are concentrated on how you can make the organization better.

"I always work to create and maintain staff passion for the organization. I share my passion with people inside the organization. I think many times leaders are really gung ho outside the organization but don't bother to exhibit that passion as they move around inside the organization. Being a leader is about being a salesperson, a cheerleader for your organization. If I don't show people that I really believe and buy into this 'product,' then why should they? I'm always looking for ways to keep the organization in the forefront and bring attention to it. I truly believe that, as a leader, I should be able at the drop of a hat, without preparation, to get up and give a speech about my organization. I should know it so well that it's a part of me. If a leader doesn't have passion for the organization, his or her communication will not be effective."

Belle Wheelan is a strong believer in the need for direct and open communication. "I have an open door all the time. If I have business that has to be done behind a closed door, I'll do it early in the morning before everybody gets there, I'll stay late at night and do it, or I'll do it at home because I need people to come in and give me information. You can't find out what's going on if you don't have information. If you're staying behind a closed door, then you are not accessible, and as the leader you should be accessible. I think the web image of leadership, where I'm in the middle but I reach out to everybody around me, depicts my style and represents a more female approach to leadership. Men are more likely to sit at the top and give information to a small group of people who, in turn, funnel it down to other people.

"As a campus president, I walked around a lot. Two thousand employees can't get to you, but you can certainly, over the course of every thirty days, get to two thousand employees. Walking around and letting people know what's going on is an important avenue for communication.

"Grapevines and gossip die when people have information because there is nothing to make up. I would much rather that people have information. Growing up, my mother always allowed me to ask questions. She didn't always answer them because sometimes it wasn't my business or she wasn't ready for me to know, but she always let me ask them. And I do that with my own staff; I let them ask questions and I give as much information as I can. Occasionally, I have to say I'm not at liberty to share that information or that's confidential. 'You might have come to a different decision, but it was my call, not yours, and this was why I made it.' When it's important that everybody understands what's going on, why a decision was made, I share information by e-mail. That way, people don't have to guess nearly as much about what's happening. I also believe that a good leader is one who'll say, 'Oops! Messed that one up. Let's try something else. You know, I used the best information I had at the time, and it just didn't pan out.' But not too often. Because when the president makes mistakes too often, it's time for the president to leave."

Belle's communication style has been described by some as blunt. In response to this characterization, in a 2002 interview with *Black Issues in Higher Education*, she describes her style as open and honest. "Bluntness is somebody who doesn't care about the impression they make. Certainly, I am very well aware of and concerned about the impression I make. But people understand that I don't play games. If you want to know what I'm thinking, then I'm going to tell you. If you don't want to know, then don't ask me.

"I've always been a go-to-the-source kind of person, not confrontational, just straightforward. If there is a problem, let's deal with it straight on. Being surreptitious has never been the way I've done business. My mother was always up-front with me. She allowed me to be up-front. I grew up that way.

"I think employees appreciate openness in their leaders. At every institution where I've worked, when I go back people still say, 'Boy, we miss you.' There's got to be something they missed other than just my silly self, and I'd like to think that part of it was the communication, taking time with people to explain things, making time for the people within the organization.

"I'm seeing many more higher education organizations create or develop the position of chief operating officer, often called an executive vice president, who is in the institution to do the day-to-day kinds of things because the role of the president has become much more external. The president has to be garnering support outside of the institution, fundraising, representing the institution to the outside constituencies and agencies. That bothers me a little bit. I'm old school enough to think that a president needs to spend time within the organization. You can't get things done if you don't have the support from the people inside. If they don't feel you are present, it is more difficult to accomplish organizational goals. In addition, you can't always depend on your immediate staff for all your information, because it will have been filtered five or six times when it finally gets to you. It's important to walk around and talk to the people on the front line, to hear the original version of the story, not the one that's been sanitized a gazillion times. If you're spending all your time outside of the institution, it is difficult to know what is really happening on the campus."

Belle's leadership skill, style, and ability served Northern Virginia Community College (NOVA) well. In 2001, *Washingtonian Magazine* included her as one of the "Top 100 Most Powerful Women in the Greater Washington Region." Her success at NOVA also drew the attention of newly elected governor of Virginia Mark Warner, who asked her to serve as his Secretary of Education. At her appointment in January 2002, he stated, "Belle's energy and willingness to build bridges between the worlds of business and education impressed me greatly. She has taken Northern Virginia by storm over the past three years with her enthusiasm, energy, and ability to get the job done."

"At about thirty years in, I was at the top of my career as president of NOVA. I didn't know what the next step was. I had community leadership experience; I had intrastate regional leadership experience. I'd been at NOVA three-and-a-half years when Governor Warner offered me the job as Secretary of Education. The position gave me an opportunity to get statewide experience.

"When you consider a leadership job, you need to sit back and say, 'Is this going to be a good fit with who I am and what my values are? Can I put up with the eighteen-hour days? Do I want to stand up in front of people all the time, be in that fishbowl, be the center of attention? Is my family comfortable constantly being out there?'

"There's a lot of stress being in that fishbowl, knowing that everywhere you go, people are looking. In my first presidency in Lynchburg, Virginia, I remember going into the liquor store just before Christmas. I had guests coming to my house and I had to replenish supplies for the holidays. A woman was coming out of the store. 'Dr. Wheelan, is this you? Well, I'm surprised to see *you* here!' she said reproachfully. Mind you, she's coming *out* of the store, but I wasn't supposed to be going in. I never went back to that liquor store. After that, I'd go to the 'hood, where people didn't care who I was. Those kinds of incidents do create a kind of internal stress that you have to learn to deal with.

"You also have to deal with the press. Every time you give a speech, you can expect that something will be taken out of context or misquoted. Then you get calls from your board chair or other officials wondering what in the world were you talking about. There is also the stress of trying to meet with 'God' and everybody in one day, dealing with budgets and reduced resources, and the list goes on. You either learn to function on five hours of sleep or adjust your day, giving up things in your personal life so that you can get some sleep and make it through those long days.

"The Presidents' Roundtable of the National Council on Black American Affairs is a group of all the African American CEOs in community colleges. At one of its workshops for people of color who aspire to the presidency, an attendee noticed that all the women presidents on the panel had short hair and asked if that was a requirement or prerequisite. Laughing, I said, 'No, but when your day starts with a breakfast meeting at 7:30 a.m. and doesn't end until 11:00 p.m. after a late dinner meeting, you had better be low maintenance. It's as simple as that. As the organizational leader you are on stage all the time. Sometimes that will mean twelve-, fifteen-, eighteen-hour days, three or four times a week. And if you can't do that, then you might want to reconsider stepping up to that leadership position.'"

In Belle's particular case, taking the job of Secretary of Education added the stress of a very long commute to the office. "I commuted a hundred miles one way for the entire four years, from Fairfax County to Richmond. My son, Reggie, was in the second semester of his senior year in high school when I took the job. I wasn't about to uproot him at that particular point. I've always been more of a night person than a morning person, so getting up at 5:30 in the morning was painful. Sometimes I got home at midnight and still had to get up at five. But, it gave me a chance to unwind and get work off my mind before I got home to Reg. So I could be Mom without work in the way. I would not recommend such a long daily commute, but you can do anything for four years [laughing]. It's kind of like writing a dissertation. It's not going to last forever.

"State policy/politics is a very different arena. If I had to do it again, I'm not sure I would take the secretary position because now I know what the job is. As a president, you can get involved in a variety of activities. I didn't feel there were as many choices in the secretary position. It's much more paper-pushing; it's much more policy, and policy only. Plus politics—a much larger percentage of it is politics. I've always been an issue person, not a partisan politics person. So there was some frustration there.

"The decision I made to take the Secretary of Education job was one not solely made for personal gain. It was one that I thought would benefit the Commonwealth. As an African American and a female, the position presented me with an opportunity to step up and make sure that the viewpoints of those groups were reflected in the education policy of the Commonwealth. Sometimes you do what's in the interest of the greater good.

"I was thirty years old before I ever met a Black woman with a Ph.D. I never want another generation of young Black women to have to go through that. So I accepted the responsibility of being a role model." She explains in an interview with *Black Issues in Higher Education*, "I am doing the best I can, trying to live up to the expectations of people who have supported me. I make myself available to others as a mentor . . . I have opened my home to many a graduate student who was writing a dissertation on leadership and women.

"The generation of women right before me was the group that opened the doors so I could walk through. It's my job to make sure those doors stay open so that more of us come through them. Whatever talents I'm perceived to have, I need to share them so that they'll continue and more people will have them."

Toward the end of Governor Warner's term, Belle accepted the offer to become the president of the Commission on Colleges of the Southern Association of Colleges and Schools (SACS). The Commission examines and accredits 798 public, private, and proprietary institutions in eleven U.S. states and Latin America. As Commission president, she works with a thirteen-member executive council that represents the seventy-seven commissioners who are elected by the member colleges. The position affords Belle the opportunity to use the leadership and management skills gained through campus experience, as well as the political skills she acquired as a member of the Virginia governor's cabinet.

Belle Wheelan is the first African American and the first woman to serve in this role. As she did at NOVA, she replaced a long-serving White male when she took the position. In 2006, Jon W. Fuller, an accreditation consultant, in an interview with the *Chronicle of Higher Education*, stated it this way, "The 'face of SACS' has changed from a Southern White man with a reputation for being pugnacious to an African American woman who has a reputation for avoiding unnecessary conflict." Officials in various organizations that have dealings with SACS were quoted as describing Belle and her appointment as "a breath of fresh air," "a particularly enlightened choice."

Wheelan took the job at a time of unprecedented challenge and change. A main source of strife was SACS's tense relations with the United Negro College Fund (UNCF) and the historically Black colleges and universities (HBCUs) in its membership. Although HBCUs make up only about thirteen percent of the institutions accredited by SACS, when Belle joined SACS, they constituted approximately one-half of the colleges that have had their accreditation withdrawn since 1989. The UNCF had charged SACS with having a racist attitude, and the organization had been very publicly embroiled in a lawsuit with Edward Waters College, a small HBCU in Jacksonville, Florida. In addition, the role of accrediting agencies, in general, was under scrutiny by the Bush administration, which called for changes described as "federalizing accreditation." Taking the job, under circumstances that "would have made many executives run the other way," Belle again demonstrated her commitment to the greater good, to giving back.

In her typical down-to-earth fashion, when Belle arrived she introduced herself to the SACS staff members saying, "I'm Belle Wheelan—Belle, as in ding-dong, Wheelan, as in wheelin' and dealin'." Belle says her good sense of humor is one of the keys to her successful leadership. "When I first joined the Rotary Club, I was in Portsmouth, Virginia. It was 1990 and membership had just opened up to women in 1988 or 1989, so there weren't many of us. I remember walking into a meeting once where I was the third woman in the room and the other two were serving food. As I walked in, a group of the men were telling a joke. When I joined the circle, they stopped. 'Don't stop,' I said. So they finished the joke, which turned out to be sexist and a bit racy. The guy telling the joke turned red, all the way down to the soles of his feet, I'm sure. I gamely one-upped him with a funnier, but less racy, joke of my own. I never had another problem with those guys in Rotary after that because they knew I had a sense of humor and that I could give as well as receive. I often use humor as a way to defuse differences and infuse my own culture into a situation.

"My cultural heritage shapes the way I lead. As an ethnic minority and a female, I'm always conscious of the fact that those are the first two things people notice about me when I walk into a room. And all of their preconceived notions or perceptions about both of those groups are going to come to the forefront before I even open my mouth. They will have judged me, unconsciously I'd like to think. But those preconceived notions will be there, ready to be validated by whatever I say.

"In 1964, when schools in Texas were integrating, I went from an all-Black Catholic school into a White high school that had only been integrated for about two years. It was a new experience for me because I had never been to school with White kids. Before I transferred to that high school, I had an eighth-grade teacher who told us it didn't matter what color our skin was because we were all Americans and "American" ended in the letters i-c-a-n, I can. She never wanted to hear us say what we couldn't do until we tried. Her guidance and advice helped me through that transition and shaped the way I think about differences today. I try not to buy into the perceptions that you might have about me, and I try not to let my perceptions about you get in the way of what I do, either. That's why the partisan politics with which I dealt while Virginia Secretary of Education drove me nuts. I wanted to deal with the issues, but it was all cluttered up with extraneous garbage, like gender, ethnicity, SES [socioeconomic status], and party affiliation. I know those are real differences, and I know that they play a part in people's points of view, but when can we not start with them [laughing]? Can't we at least start with the basic issue and then see how others are impacted by it?

"Being a child of the sixties, living through two revolutions, a Black revolution and a women's revolution, I grew up with the belief that there isn't a door that can't be opened. There's nothing I can't do, and I can do it better than most men in half the time. It's important that a woman who wants to be a leader has that level of self-confidence. The belief that, with a little heart and a lot of learning, I can do anything.

"The career opportunities for women today are unending. There are so many new fields. When I talk to elementary school children, I remind them that it hasn't been twenty years that we've had ATMs, cell phones, or laptop computers. New fields are opening up every day, and we need people who can design, build, and repair. Women should be prepared, keep their options open, and not write off any job just because they hadn't considered it before. The sky's the limit.

"For women who want to work in higher education, more opportunities for college presidencies are becoming available, especially in community colleges, because a large number of those colleges started in the 1960s, and the staff that started them are retiring. Colleges have tended to promote vice presidents to presidents, and the vice presidents are as old as the presidents," she laughs. "That traditional talent pool is shrinking. Women can now go in and fill those positions, from faculty to dean to vice president to president.

"Generally, however, for women, career choices still revolve more around family than they do for men: whether to have a family or not, whether you're going to have a long-distance or commuter relationship, will you uproot the children? Those kinds of decisions are choices that two generations ago, probably even one generation ago, women didn't have to think about nearly as much because the career choices weren't there. Women still have the major responsibility of childbearing and -raising, whether you have a career or not. We still are traditional enough in this country that most women will follow the husband's job opportunities. We don't have nearly as many husbands following their wives. It's getting better, but that is still an issue.

"I have been a single parent since Reggie was ten months old. It wasn't easy to have a career and raise a child at the same time, making sure homework got done, dinner got fixed, going to football games, and everything else so that he could have as normal a life as possible. It made for very long days.

"My motto during his childhood was, take one day at a time. During his early elementary school years, the YMCA before- and after-school program was a lifesaver. I would barter for child care with neighbors, taking their children one night, if they could take Reggie another. Some years, his father would keep him every other weekend and one month in the summer, which provided occasional long-term relief. But Reggie attended a fair share of rubber chicken lunches and dinners with me and he met a lot of people. It worked well for us. We bonded closely, and I'm not sure we would have done so if he had had two parents at home. He's twenty-three and works and goes to school in the Washington, D.C., area. He's been in the public eye all of his life. Now he is old enough to appreciate the contacts that he's made because of the jobs that I've held.

"When Reggie turned twenty-one, it was liberating. I got to be spontaneous again. I realized I didn't have to rush home. I could decide at the last minute to stay late at work or have dinner out with a friend. When you want to have a fulfilling personal life, as well as a professional life, it makes for very long days. Periodically, you do have to step back and remember who you are and why you signed on for this role in the first place. Leaders occasionally need to check themselves to see, 'Am I still enjoying this? Am I still doing the job well? Is this still a good fit for me?' It is important to do this type of reflection because if you lose yourself, your family will suffer, you will suffer, the organization will suffer."

Like most effective leaders who have enjoyed long-term success, Belle has discovered what it is she needs to maintain her stamina and energy. "I love music; I live with it. I listen to music in the car, in the office. I'll walk up and down the hall singing because, for me, music does soothe the savage beast. I also catch up on sleep on the weekends. I read fiction. I'll go the bookstore and spend a hundred dollars on trash novels that I'll go through in two weeks. I get my nails done every two weeks and I've started getting pedicures. I try to remember that I, too, am a person and I need to take time for me."

Surprisingly, when she was working in Richmond, her long commute, though tiring, had its rewards. "The drive was against the traffic and interstate all the way. I would put on the CDs, the cruise control, and talk on the phone. I actually had more time for my friends because I was on the road for an hour and forty minutes. I called people that I hadn't talked to in ages. So from that standpoint, it allowed me to have more of a personal life than I had before. When I had a three-minute or a three-mile commute, as soon as I got home, I was doing something else and just didn't stop and take that kind of time." As Virginia's Secretary of Education, Belle also found it renewing to step away from the job once in a while and "visit schools, to remind myself why I was putting up with all the paperwork and the legislative politics.

"Backing away helps me guard against burnout. I think that's probably why I've changed jobs as often as I have. You get to a point as president of an institution when you have gone through five budget cycles, you have gone through five faculty evaluations, and that's enough. For some people it's maybe ten. Whatever, the routine gets to you and you look for new challenges. Sometimes feeling burnout comes from overcommitting yourself, not knowing how to say no. When I became president at Lynchburg, I was the first Black woman to be a college president in Virginia, so every woman's group and every minority group asked me to be one of their speakers and I would say yes. Plus I'm just a big ham. I missed the classroom, and here was an audience who thought I knew what I was talking about. 'This is wonderful! Sure, heck yeah, I want to be center stage' [laughing].

"Well, I'm at a point now, because I've been out here long enough, that it's okay for somebody else to fill that need. I've learned to say, 'Gosh, I'd love to, but I just really can't. I'm sorry, I have something else scheduled.' What I have scheduled might be getting my nails done or grocery shopping. Now, believe me, I still do my fair share of speeches, but I guard my weekends and evenings as much as I possibly can because I need time for me. I need downtime. I just can't keep pushing. As a leader, if you're not at your best, then you're not going to do your best and the organization suffers. It is a difficult lesson to learn when you are a helping kind of person and you feel the responsibility of being a role model.

"Presidents and other organizational leaders sometimes get caught up in being the official spokesperson because leaders can be control freaks. A real leader doesn't need credit, doesn't always need to be out front. Through maturity and experience, an effective leader learns that sometimes it doesn't matter who gets the credit as long as the job gets done. It can even be my idea, but I don't have to get the credit. I've gotten my glory in a similar situation before. Let somebody else have the glory this time.

"Delegation was probably the toughest skill for me to learn, because I knew if I did whatever it was, it was going to get done the way I wanted it, when I wanted it, in the manner I wanted it. The ability to delegate is something into which you have to grow if you are going to be successful. Nobody else in the organization grows if you do everything yourself. I had to learn how to let go. The benefit of doing so is that it's very rewarding when you can see not only that your organization is flourishing but also that the people in it are flourishing as well. It's a good feeling to know that you had a little something to do with that.

"The work environment is a relationship between you and the people who work in the organization. I don't have to like the people I work with, and I don't have to have them like me. But I do have to have them believe me and trust me when I tell them something and vice versa. Credibility is the most important attribute that a leader needs to be effective. If people can't take what you say to the bank, then they're not going to follow you. In order to maintain your position as a leader, people have to believe that you mean what you say and that you say what you mean, that they can trust you.

"My approach when I move into an organization is to trust everybody till they give me reason not to. If you are skeptical of everybody, I think it is uncomfortable for you and your employees and difficult to settle into a relationship of trust. It has worked much better for me over the years to trust going in. It makes it easier to get the job done. However, once they break that trust, it's broken. If there is no trust, no credibility, then it is time for someone to go.

"If someone on my administrative team isn't working out, I've usually been able to either move that person into a different position or help him or her find a job someplace else. I think that sometimes people are in the wrong job because the position has changed since they got it and they just aren't the right fit anymore. Or they've been in the job too long and they've gotten bored with it and they need some encouragement to go do something different.

"Some of the most difficult decisions that leaders make are related to personnel. Most of my best decisions have been around people. During my presidency at NOVA, I took a risk by hiring two people who didn't have any experience in higher education. They came from a different organizational sector but had the skills that I thought we needed to move the institution forward. Although some people were skeptical when I hired them, they both did, indeed, work out very well for the institution. I think one of my strengths is my ability to judge people and their fit for an organization.

"Probably the worst decision I made was also a personnel decision. When I was president at Central Virginia Community College, I moved a faculty member into an administrative position, a grant position. Unfortunately this person didn't have and never developed any fund management skills and ended up mismanaging the funds because of poor record-keeping and accounting. It wasn't theft, just bad management. That was a bad decision on my part, and I really struggled with it.

"I had never fired anybody until I became Secretary of Education. It was awful. The person I fired was misusing state equipment and state funds. I would have gone to bat for her, but she had no remorse. She gave my office as a reference a couple of times and I couldn't recommend her for another job. I feel badly about it, but she did it to herself. Firing someone is the last resort for me. I've seen presidents fire people just because they could. 'I don't like you, it's time for you to go, you work at my will, so goodbye.' Such behavior bothers me.

"We have to work as a well-oiled team. The whole organization depends on everybody working together. An effective leader has to learn to build a team and at the same time respect the individuality of the people on the team. I've always inherited an initial team. It's more of a challenge to lead a team when you inherit it than it is if you can bring in your own people. But if we can agree on a timeline and a desired outcome, I don't hassle people if they approach the task differently from how I would, as long as it works. Having moved from organization to organization, I understand that different people have different ways of doing things."

A sign on her desk reads, "Leadership isn't all glory." Glory doesn't seem to be a driving force behind Belle's desire to be a leader or her success in each leadership endeavor she's undertaken. Expanding horizons, opening doors, providing opportunities, showing the way, all for the greater good. That's what Belle Wheelan is all about.

BIBLIOGRAPHICAL NOTE

This chapter about Belle Wheelan derives from in-depth interviews, her vitae and bio (retrieved June 10, 2008, from http://www.sacscoc.org/president.asp), and several publications and websites. These include:

Bollag, B. (2006, June 2). Trying prevention before punishment. *The Chronicle of Higher Education*. Retrieved June 10, 2008, from http://chronicle.com

Chenoweth, K., Stephens, A., & Evelyn, J. (1998, May 28). Powerful sisters. *Black Issues in Higher Education, 15*(7).

Jeff, C. (2007, November 3). Advice to leaders: Listen, ask, laugh. *The Free Lance-Star*. Retrieved June 20, 2008, from http://www.fredericksburg.com

Licensed to lead; Dr. Belle S. Wheelan, former president of Northern Virginia Community College, leads Virginia's Department of Education. Special report: Women in higher education. Interview. (2002, March 28). *Black Issues in Higher Education, 19*(3).

nine

SIX Cs OF LEADERSHIP

T HE STORIES OF THE seven women featured in this book are
clearly stories of leadership. They live it. They study it. They
are experts on leadership. And, although each one puts her own
unique spin on it, they consistently identify caring, confidence,
competence, communication, credibility, and a sense of calling
as fundamental elements of leadership.

Caring manifests itself in passion for what they do and the organizations they lead. Belle Wheelan contends, "As a leader having
passion for an organization means that everywhere you go, it's the
first topic of conversation. Being a leader is about being a salesperson, a cheerleader for your organization. If I don't show people
that I really believe and buy into this 'product,' then why should
they?" Jerry Sue Thornton cares "deeply about community colleges" and Cuyahoga. "I have a passion for education. People hear
my passion, they see it. It's in everything I do." Marvalene Hughes
adds, "It was that passion that gave me the extra adrenalin on
which to operate during the crisis [of Hurricane Katrina]."

Caring also surfaces in a desire to give back to other women,
to other African American women, to African Americans. Their
values took root in the 1960s, a time of strong cohesion in the
Black community, a time during which African Americans and
women made great strides toward equality. Grateful for the
support they have received, these women leaders express a need

to give back to those communities that nourished their growth and leadership. Marvalene Hughes helped found the Millennium Leadership Initiative and has worked tirelessly to lead Dillard University back from the brink after Hurricane Katrina. A graduate of a historically Black institution, she admits, "I became aware that I wasn't giving back to the African American culture to the extent that I wanted." Dillard gave her an opportunity to act on that desire. Yolanda Moses has always had a "very strong commitment to inclusivity and social justice." Lois Carson's entire career has been devoted to community, community action, and promoting social change. The Southeast Asian Peoples Farm Project is a prime example. She also believes that being a role model is critical, "I love to work with younger women, to be a role model, to help them." As does Belle Wheelan, who says, "The generation of women right before me was the group that opened the doors so I could walk through. It's my job to make sure those doors stay open so that more of us come through them." She adds, "I am doing the best I can, trying to live up to the expectations of people who have supported me." Several of the women in this book donate their time and energy to the Millennium Leadership Initiative, the New Presidents Academy, and other leadership and mentoring programs.

Austin, Carson, Hughes, Moses, Tatum, Thornton, and Wheelan exude confidence. In essence they all agree that by the time someone comes into an executive leadership role they should be self-aware, self-disciplined, and self-confident, or they won't succeed. Marvalene Hughes suggests that "a good foundation" of varied experiences helps to develop confidence. Jerry Sue Thornton says, "You have to be assertive and have the confidence to move forward. It has to be a part of who you are, a part of your fabric." As Beverly Tatum puts it, "Who could do this job without some sense of confidence?"

Confidence, at least in part, arises from competence. Beverly Tatum states, "Clearly, as a leader, I must be competent, particularly as a Black woman. I can be as passionate as I want to, but if I'm incompetent, I'm not going anywhere." Marvalene Hughes strongly agrees: "Being competent is essential. I'm not at the stage where I do this now, but I used to deliberately reflect on what competency means in the academic community, and what one has to do in order to bridge from one role to the next." Debra Austin contends, "Competence has to show through. Some individuals get by for a very short period on charisma and charm. They are usually great communicators, and they can mobilize people, but there is no substance."

Throughout their stories, communication takes on all sorts of shapes and forms, but what is highly evident across these women is their determination to gather information. They value and seek out information from a variety of sources. Belle Wheelan opines, "You can't find out what's going on if you don't have information." They are committed to an open-door policy and "management by walking around." Wheelan's door is open all the time: "If I have business that has to be done behind a closed door, I'll do it early in the morning before everybody gets there, I'll stay late at night and do it, or I'll do it at home because I need people to come in and give me information. In addition she agrees that, "Walking around and letting people know what's going on is an important avenue for communication." Jerry Sue Thornton uses it as a way of identifying what she calls "itches" in the organization. "I have lots of conversations with students and staff. People appreciate that I value their opinions and that I'm interested."

They speak about listening and watching. Beverly Tatum reads people. Debra Austin watches body language. Jerry Sue Thornton suspects that "minorities and women are sometimes good at this because we have had to study people; we've had to understand people better. There is no choice. If you don't have the power, you have to think about how the people that you work and interface with think and act in order to get your job done. As minorities we've had to watch and understand those in power a lot more than they've ever had to watch and understand us. It's a given. You do it to survive."

Communication, confidence, competence, and the belief of others that you care, all affect credibility. Hughes, Austin, and Wheelan tell us that if you don't establish credibility, you are destined for difficulty. From Marvalene Hughes we learned the importance of trustworthiness and integrity. She says, "Inauthenticity creates mistrust, a lack of credibility, and disbelief." Beverly Tatum agrees stating, "People have to trust their leaders. You have to have integrity." As Belle Wheelan puts it, "If people can't take what you say to the bank, then they're not going to follow you."

None of these women denies the importance of caring, confidence, competence, communication, and credibility; but what really seems to drive them, pushing them into leadership positions, is a sense of calling. They are born leaders. "I have always believed that through leadership I can help, I am making contributions to this world," Debra Austin declares. Lois Carson and Jerry Sue Thornton both firmly believe that they are doing the job they were born to do.

They are all certain that they are part of a larger purpose. They perceive higher education leadership to be a mission that guides their lives. "In 1991, I had a spiritual awakening that has informed my choices ever since," said Beverly Tatum. When Marvalene Hughes accepted the presidency of Dillard University, she had no idea of the major role she would play in its future. But she felt called to the institution. "I knew that this was meant to be the next stage in my life." The granddaughter of a Baptist minister, Jerry Sue Thornton declared, "I chose to go into education because it's a ministry for me. Higher education—and especially community college education—is a calling."

This sense of calling is more than enthusiasm and passion for higher education. At an early age, Lois Carson learned from the nuns at her school that her leadership skills were "a gift from God and you have to use them." Marvalene Hughes believes that spirituality is a crucial dimension of leadership: "The presidency is quite demanding, and I know that there is more than my physical body engaged in all this complex activity. There is something that guides me in the universe." She adds, "You are not all alone as you lead an organization." Beverly Tatum agrees: "A sense of calling helps generate the stamina, energy, and resilience you need to do the job."

Someone once said, "A life without cause is a life without effect." We add that the effect must be the result of meaningful response to the call for action implicit in the cause. For several decades, researchers and commentators on higher education have called for more African American women in leadership roles to serve as role models for the increasing number of women and minorities entering higher education and to bring a needed diversity of thought, experience, and perspective to higher education leadership.

Call and response.[1] The seven women in this book have heard the call to leadership and responded. They have found that higher education leadership "is not just a job, it truly is a calling." And, as Beverly Tatum says, "responding to that call has been deeply satisfying."

---

1. Call and response is spontaneous interaction in which statements or calls from the sender are punctuated by expressions/actions or responses by the receiver. Call and response is an organizing concept used in African American public speaking, religious observance, and music and is familiar to all within this community.

ten

PROJECT METHODOLOGY

THE STORIES PRESENTED in this volume are part of an ongoing qualitative research project begun in 2002 by a team of women academics from a variety of disciplines, including business, education, sports, public administration, and hospitality. We recognized, as various sources have documented, that, despite the progress of women in the general workforce, women continue to be underrepresented in each of our fields of study. Much of the literature about and research on leadership has been written by and about men, primarily White men. In addition, leadership has traditionally been examined using male behaviors and characteristics as the norm against which women are assessed. The leadership literature presents mixed messages about whether women leaders function differently from men who hold comparable leadership positions. We believe that the issue is really effectiveness rather than gender, and that effective leaders, male or female, subscribe to similar beliefs about leadership and act more similarly than differently when they enact those roles.

Our extensive investigation of the leadership literature in our fields found the body of knowledge on leadership to be disjointed, with some researchers investigating a particular approach to leadership (e.g., transformational leadership) and others examining a completely different, but equally important, aspect crucial to effective leadership (e.g., cognitive framing). Based on our assumption that effective leadership is not gender-specific, we synthesized existing literature into a series of nine tenets of effective leadership (see Table 10.1). This created a basic structure about what we believe contributes to effective leadership.

We purposely selected participants for their ability to inform the study (Lincoln & Guba, 1985; Merriam, 1998; Yin, 2003). These women were viewed as effective leaders using two general estimates of effectiveness: reputation among peers and length of experience. In addition, we strove for ethnic, geographic, and institutional diversity within each field. The women chosen for the study also had control over organizational budgets and more than five employees who report directly to them.

TABLE 10.1
Nine Tenets of Effective Leadership

Effective leaders are passionate about their organizations. They exhibit extraordinary commitment not only to the organization but to its people.

Effective leaders are reflective. They are self-aware, self-disciplined, self-confident, and self-assured.

Effective leaders are competent. They possess the intelligence and mental capacity to get the job done.

Effective leaders are great communicators. They have their finger on the pulse of the organization.

Effective leaders understand the role that culture plays in shaping the way they lead.

Effective leaders possess the physical and emotional stamina, energy, and resilience needed to persevere in the long run.

Effective leaders are focused yet forward thinking.

Effective leaders respect and value individuality.

Effective leaders possess credibility. The building blocks of credibility are trust, integrity, and power.

Because leadership is affected by context, it is difficult to study a leader independent of context. Therefore, we chose qualitative case study as an appropriate methodology for the project (Yin, 2003). Case study design enabled the researchers to compare the leaders across organizational types, looking for common threads and patterns in their responses (Babbie, 2001; Miles & Huberman, 1994; Yin, 2003). A semistructured interview protocol was developed and piloted before the participant interviews (Lincoln & Guba, 1985; Miles & Huberman, 1994; Yin, 2003). Most of the interviews were conducted face-to-face and took two to four hours to complete. All were tape-recorded and transcribed. Data were categorized systematically by themes and patterns of responses delineated by multiple researchers to ensure consistency and validity. Researchers also gathered additional information pertaining to each leader and her organization for the case studies via college documents, newspaper articles, and the Internet. Once the cases were written, the research team reviewed them, and each case was shared with its respective participant for accuracy and trustworthiness.

Although other reports of this research focus on the leaders' experiences in relationship to the tenets of effective leadership, the work presented in the "Journeys to Leadership" series presents these women's individual and unique voices as they discuss their values and the events that have shaped them as leaders in their respective fields.

REFERENCES

Babbie, E. (2001). *The practice of social research* (9th ed.). Belmont, CA: Wadsworth/Thomson Learning, Inc.
Lincoln, Y. S., & Guba, E. G. (1985). *Naturalistic inquiry.* Newbury Park, CA: Sage

Merriam, S. B. (1998). *Qualitative research and case study applications in education.* San Francisco: Jossey-Bass.

Miles, M. B., & Huberman, A. M. (1994). *Qualitative data analysis* (2nd ed.). Thousand Oaks, CA: Sage.

Yin, R. K. (2003). *Case study research: Design and methods.* Thousand Oaks, CA: Sage.

INDEX

accessibility: Carson on, 36; Hughes on, 55; Tatum on, 89

accreditation: Austin on, 20; Wheelan on, 131–132

ACE. *See* American Council on Education

Adams, Anneli, 25–37

American Anthropological Association, 72

American Association for Higher Education, 73

American Association of State Colleges and Universities, 41–42

American Association of University Professors, 114

American Council on Education (ACE), 72, 117

anthropology, Moses on, 61, 65–66

antiracist education, Tatum on, 77

Arizona State University, 51

Association of Community College Trustees, Board of, 29–30

Austin, Debra, 8*f*, 9–23

Austin, Kenneth, 11

Bawek, James F., 71–72

Bethune, Gordon, 108

Bryant, Castell, 18

burnout, Wheelan on, 136–137

California Community College system, 29, 36

California Leadership Development Program, 62

California State Polytechnic University–Pomona, 62–64

California State University: Dominguez Hills, 64; Stanislaus, 39–41

calling, 146–147; Hughes on, 49–50, 65; Tatum on, 77

caring, 143–144. *See also* passion

Carson, Lois, 24*f*, 25–37

Catholicism: Carson on, 27–28; Tatum on, 79; Wheelan on, 122

CCNY. *See* City College of New York

Centenary College, 44

Central Virginia Community College, 123

Champion for Justice Award, 35

child care: Carson on, 29, 34; Wheelan on, 135

City College of New York (CCNY), 66–71

~ 153 ~

Index

Index